URBAN AND AMISH

URBAN AND AMISH

Classic Quilts and Modern Updates

MYRA HARDER

Martingale®
Create with Confidence

DEDICATION

This book is dedicated to my parents, Bernie and Betty Klassen, who took me to distant countries and cultures, and who taught me that you can learn many lessons outside of the classroom.

And to my husband, Mark, and our children, Samson and Robyn, who have made every family trip a true adventure.

Urban and Amish: Classic Quilts and Modern Updates
© 2014 by Myra Harder

Martingale®
19021 120th Ave. NE, Ste. 102
Bothell, WA 98011-9511 USA
ShopMartingale.com

Printed in China
19 18 17 16 15 14   8 7 6 5 4 3 2 1

Library of Congress Cataloging-in-Publication Data
is available upon request.

ISBN: 978-1-60468-456-8

MISSION STATEMENT
Dedicated to providing quality products and service to inspire creativity.

CREDITS

PUBLISHER AND CHIEF VISIONARY OFFICER:
   Jennifer Erbe Keltner

EDITOR IN CHIEF: Mary V. Green

DESIGN DIRECTOR: Paula Schlosser

MANAGING EDITOR: Karen Costello Soltys

ACQUISITIONS EDITOR: Karen M. Burns

TECHNICAL EDITOR: Nancy Mahoney

COPY EDITOR: Sheila Chapman Ryan

PRODUCTION MANAGER: Regina Girard

COVER AND INTERIOR DESIGNER: Adrienne Smitke

PHOTOGRAPHER: Brent Kane

ILLUSTRATOR: Lisa Lauch

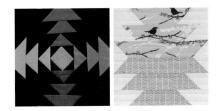

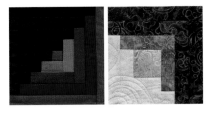

CONTENTS

THE PROJECTS

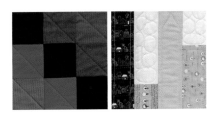

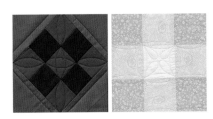

INTRODUCTION

Working on *Urban and Amish* has been a great journey. I love seeing the designs and fabrics come together to form both traditional and new quilts. This book is truly as close as I have come to having quilts reflect who I am: the urban quilts represent my love of the bold fabrics currently available, but the Amish quilts take me back to where it all started.

For a few years in my childhood, my parents' work brought our family from Canada to Lancaster County, Pennsylvania. Those years made a lasting impression on my life. While we were there, Amish women taught my mother to quilt—and quilting came into my life as well.

My family got to know several Amish families, and through these new friendships I was invited into the Amish world. I spent countless weekends working and playing on their beautiful farmyards. I came to love helping out with the chores, and when we had time to play, we would spend it on trampolines, in haylofts, riding horses, swimming in ponds, catching fireflies, and eating Turkey Hill ice cream. There was always so much to do that you never missed having a television around. I quickly came to realize that the lives of the Amish were full and fulfilled.

The simple styles of Amish quilts harmonize with their way of life. The Amish have been wearing the same style of clothing in muted colors for generations, and their choices in clothing and quilts reflect their plain and unadorned lifestyle. The most important aspect of the Amish life is their faith, which is seen in how they truly care for their families and friends.

The urban quilts in this book are inspired by their traditional Amish counterparts. Starting with classic designs, I created quilts that had a bold, modern feel. I purposely created blocks and layouts that used large pieces of fabrics so that the beautiful prints could be seen. The quilt layout is almost secondary to the fabrics that are used. The fabrics tell most of the story and set the tone for what the finished quilt will look like. These urban quilts use a wide variety of prints and many different color combinations, which make them very compatible with different homes and tastes.

Throughout the book, I believe you'll be able to tie each urban quilt back to its Amish inspiration. For me, even as I grow and design in new modern ways, I remember where my roots are.

~Myra

AMISH FABRICS

If look closely, you will find a variety of color palettes in Amish quilts. It was common for Amish communities in different states to adopt their own set of colors. For example, the Amish quilts from my area of Lancaster County, Pennsylvania, didn't have a lot of black in them. Instead, you'd see navy used as the darkest color. However, if you traveled west to Ohio and Indiana, you'd find many Amish quilts that *do* feature black as a main color. True experts in Amish quilts can often identify which Amish community made the quilt depending on the colors used. With the projects in this book, I tried to touch on palettes that are used in various areas and not just those from Lancaster County.

One of my favorite reference books is *Amish Wall Quilts* by Rachel Thomas Pellman (Martingale, 2001). If you're interested in knowing more about the Amish life and their quilts, I highly recommend this book. Rachel lives in Lancaster County, in the heart of Amish country, and she's done a wonderful job documenting the different color palettes that are used by various groups of Amish. I referred to her expertise in choosing appropriate colors for the Amish quilts in this book. The one exception would be the pear green that I used in a few of the projects. This isn't a color that's found in traditional Amish quilts; however, I remember many of the young Amish girls having dresses in this color, and I wanted to include that memory—and the splash of color.

■ *Examples of colors often found in Amish quilts, plus my own addition of the bright pear green (bottom).*

URBAN FABRICS

Some of today's most popular fabrics are large, bold, and irresistible. You'll find that often, fabric designs are larger than they were a few years ago, and these new large-scale prints need new quilt designs. We now create quilts that use fabrics in large pieces and challenge traditional design elements. We're also seeing color combinations that are as striking as the print size. The new colors are tied closely to the fashion industry and we're "dressing" our homes with these hues.

Quilters want to create quilts simply because of the beautiful bold prints that are now available. With these new fabrics, even a very simple layout can look fresh and modern.

Many of today's fabrics are created in collections where all of the prints and colors work together. If you're looking for fabrics that will complement each other, it's easiest to look for prints from the same collection. When you find a modern print you love, it's fun to look a little further and find out what other fabrics have been created by the same designer. Some designers have even developed their own specific color palettes, and their fabrics become easily identifiable because of the colors they do—and don't—use.

A new favorite practice among modern quilters is working with precut fabrics—2½"-wide strips, 10" squares, and 5" squares. These packages of fabric allow us to use a wide variety of prints without having to purchase a lot of yardage. Some of the projects in this book will work great with these precut fabrics. A few others use 2½"-wide strips or 5" squares, but really don't require an entire package of precuts. Of course, if you don't use every square in a charm pack, simply add those extras to your stash. You can also cut your own sets of strips and squares from scraps, keeping them on hand for easy use in future projects.

■ *Some of the large-scale prints used in Chinese Lanterns, page 15.*

■ "Pineapple," pieced by Myra Harder and quilted by Katie Friesen

PINEAPPLE

After years of being back in Canada, my family took a trip back to Pennsylvania to visit our Amish friends. During this trip, I saw a quilt displayed in a quilt-shop window in the small Amish town of Intercourse that made me want to learn to quilt. It was a Pineapple wall hanging, and I thought it was the most beautiful quilt I'd ever seen.

Why are we drawn into quilting by the most difficult projects? I learned to quilt with a few easier projects, but now I have the skill to create an Amish Pineapple.

- **FINISHED QUILT**
  51½" x 51½"

- **FINISHED BLOCK**
  12" x 12"

AMISH TO URBAN
See "Chinese Lanterns" on page 15 for an urban twist on this Amish quilt.

MATERIALS

Yardage is based on 42"-wide fabric.

3¼ yards of black solid for blocks, outer border, and binding
¼ yard *each* of 9 assorted solids for blocks
⅓ yard of blue solid for inner border
⅛ yard of olive-green solid for blocks
3¼ yards of fabric for backing
56" x 56" piece of batting

CUTTING

From the *lengthwise* grain of the black solid, cut:
2 strips, 6½" x 51½"
2 strips, 6½" x 39½"
18 squares, 6" x 6"; cut the squares in half diagonally to yield
        36 triangles

From the *crosswise* grain of the remaining black solid, cut:
1 strip, 2" x 42"; crosscut into 18 squares, 2" x 2". Cut the squares
        in half diagonally to yield 36 triangles.
22 strips, 1½" x 42"; crosscut into:
        36 rectangles, 1½" x 7½"
        36 rectangles, 1½" x 6"
        36 rectangles, 1½" x 5"
        36 rectangles, 1½" x 3½"
6 strips, 2½" x 42"

From the olive-green solid, cut:
9 squares, 1⅞" x 1⅞"

From *each* of the assorted solids, cut:
2 strips, 1½" x 42"; crosscut into:
        4 rectangles, 1½" x 6½" (36 total)
        4 rectangles, 1½" x 5½" (36 total)
        4 rectangles, 1½" x 4½" (36 total)
        4 rectangles, 1½" x 3½" (36 total)
2 squares, 2½" x 2½"; cut the squares in half diagonally to yield
        4 triangles (36 total)

From the blue solid, cut:
2 strips, 2" x 39½"
2 strips, 2" x 36½"

MAKING THE BLOCKS

The most important part of making a Pineapple block is to be as accurate as possible, because the block grows with each round. This is one of the few times that I trim the blocks after each round is added. For each block, choose four different solid colors. From each color, you'll use one triangle and one of each rectangle size.

1. Sew black 2" triangles to opposite sides of an olive-green square. Press the seam allowances toward the triangles. Sew black 2" triangles to the two remaining sides of the square. Press the seam allowances toward the triangles. Trim the unit, making sure to leave ¼" beyond the points of the olive-green square for seam allowances.

2. Sew a different solid-color triangle to each side of the unit from step 1. Press the seam allowances toward each newly added triangle. Trim the unit, making sure to leave ¼" beyond the points of the black square for seam allowances.

3. Sew a black 1½" x 3½" rectangle to each side of the unit from step 2. Press the seam allowances toward each newly added rectangle. Trim the unit, making sure to leave ¼" beyond the points of the colored triangles for seam allowances.

4. Sew solid-color 1½" x 3½" rectangles to the sides of the unit as shown. Press the seam allowances toward each newly added rectangle. Trim the rectangles even with the edges of the black pieces.

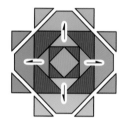
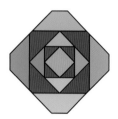

5. Sew black 1½" x 5" rectangles to the sides of the unit as shown. Press the seam allowances toward each newly added rectangle. Trim the rectangles even with the edges of the solid-color rectangles. The unit should measure 8½" x 8½".

6. Sew solid-color 1½" x 4½" rectangles to the sides of the unit as shown. Press the seam allowances toward each newly added rectangle. Trim the rectangles even with the edges of the black rectangles.

7. Sew black 1½" x 6" rectangles to the sides of the unit as shown. Press the seam allowances toward each newly added rectangle. Trim the rectangles even with the edges of the solid-color rectangles.

8. Sew solid-color 1½" x 5½" rectangles to the sides of the unit as shown. Press the seam allowances toward each newly added rectangle. Trim the rectangles even with the edges of the black rectangles.

 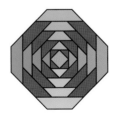

9. Sew black 1½" x 7½" rectangles to the sides of the unit as shown. Press the seam allowances toward each newly added rectangle. Trim the rectangles even with the edges of the solid-color rectangles.

10. Sew solid-color 1½" x 6½" rectangles to the sides of the unit as shown. Press the seam allowances toward each newly added rectangle. Trim the rectangles even with the edges of the black rectangles.

 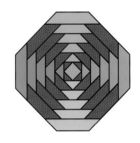

11. Sew black 6" triangles to the corners of the unit as shown. Press the seam allowances toward the black triangles. Trim the triangles even with the edges of the solid-color rectangles. The block should measure 12½" x 12½".

12. Repeat steps 1–11 to make a total of nine blocks.

ASSEMBLING THE QUILT TOP

1. Lay out the blocks in three rows of three blocks each. Join the blocks into rows. Press the seam allowances in opposite directions from row to row. Join the rows and press the seam allowances in one direction. The quilt top should measure 36½" x 36½".

2. Sew the blue 36½"-long strips to opposite sides of the quilt top. Press the seam allowances toward the blue strips. Sew the blue 39½"-long strips to the top and bottom of the quilt top to complete the inner border. Press the seam allowances toward the inner border.

3. Sew the black 39½"-long strips to opposite sides of the quilt top. Press the seam allowances toward the black strips. Sew the black 51½"-long strips to the top and bottom of the quilt top to complete the outer border. Press the seam allowances toward the outer border.

FINISHING THE QUILT

For detailed instructions on finishing techniques, refer to "Finishing Your Quilt" on page 77.

1. Cut and piece the backing fabric so it's 3" to 6" larger than the quilt top. Layer the quilt top with batting and backing. Baste the layers together.

2. Hand or machine quilt as desired. See "Quilting Suggestions" below.

3. Square up the quilt sandwich.

4. Use the black 2½"-wide strips to make and attach the binding.

QUILTING SUGGESTIONS

Staying true to its Amish influence, this project was quilted in a very traditional manner. Using black thread, straight lines were quilted in the ditch and a continuous feather design was quilted around the wide outer border.

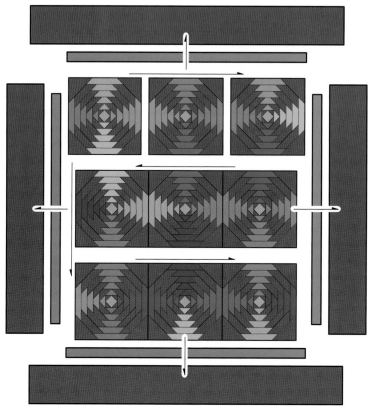

Quilt assembly

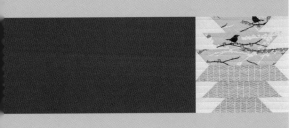

CHINESE LANTERNS

If there's one fabric designer I admire, it's Joel Dewberry. Joel creates stunning prints that combine great scale with fresh color palettes.

My inspiration for this quilt came after attending a friend's beautiful wedding, where we released colorful Chinese lanterns into the night sky. That image stayed with me as I created this quilt. The size of this new block lets me show off some of my favorite prints from my favorite designer. And now I finally have the perfect "Joel Dewberry" quilt for my collection.

- **FINISHED QUILT**
  75½" x 90½"

- **FINISHED BLOCK**
  15" x 15"

URBAN TO AMISH
See "Pineapple" on page 11 for the Amish inspiration for this urban quilt.

MATERIALS

Yardage is based on 42"-wide fabric.

5½ yards of white print for blocks
½ yard *each* of 10 assorted prints for blocks*
¾ yard of dark-red fabric for binding
5½ yards of fabric for backing
80" x 95" piece of batting

*You can make 3 blocks from each print.

CUTTING

From the white print, cut:
60 strips, 3" x 42"; crosscut into:
    30 rectangles, 3" x 15½"
    60 rectangles, 3" x 8"
    60 rectangles, 3" x 6¾"
    60 rectangles, 3" x 5½"
    60 rectangles, 3" x 4¼"
    60 squares, 3" x 3"

From *each* of the assorted prints, cut:
5 strips, 3" x 42"; crosscut into:
    3 rectangles, 3" x 15½" (30 total)
    3 rectangles, 3" x 13" (30 total)
    3 rectangles, 3" x 10½" (30 total)
    3 rectangles, 3" x 8" (30 total)
    3 rectangles, 3" x 5½" (30 total)

From the dark-red fabric, cut:
9 strips, 2½" x 42"

■ "Chinese Lanterns," pieced by Myra Harder and quilted by Katie Friesen

MAKING THE BLOCKS

The blocks are assembled in six rows. A white 3" x 15½" rectangle is used for row 1. Rows 2–6 are constructed from two white rectangles or squares and one print rectangle

1. Place a white 3" x 8" rectangle on the right end of a print 3" x 5½" rectangle, right sides together and raw edges aligned as shown. Draw a line on the wrong side of the white rectangle 3" up and 3" over from the corner as shown. Stitch on the marked diagonal line. Trim the excess corner fabric, leaving a ¼" seam allowance. Flip the pieces open and press the seam allowances toward the print rectangle.

2. Place a white 3" x 8" rectangle on the left end of the unit from step 1, right sides together and raw edges aligned as shown. Draw a line on the wrong side of the white rectangle as in step 1. Stitch, trim, and press the pieces in the same manner as before to complete row 2.

Row 2

3. Repeat steps 1 and 2 using two white 3" x 6¾" rectangles and one print 3" x 8" rectangle as shown to make row 3.

 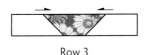

Row 3

4. Repeat steps 1 and 2 using two white 3" x 5½" rectangles and one print 3" x 10½" rectangle as shown to make row 4.

Row 4

5. Repeat steps 1 and 2 using two white 3" x 4¼" rectangles and one print 3" x 13" rectangle as shown to make row 5.

Row 5

6. Repeat steps 1 and 2 using two white 3" squares and one print 3" x 15½" rectangle as shown to make row 6.

Row 6

7. Lay out a white 3" x 15½" rectangle and rows 2–6 as shown. Join the rows to make one block. Press the seam allowances in one direction.

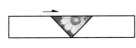

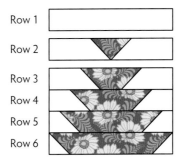

8. Repeat steps 1–7 to make a total of 30 blocks.

ASSEMBLING THE QUILT TOP

1. Lay out the block in six rows of five blocks each, rotating every other block 180° to form lanterns as shown in the quilt assembly diagram below.

2. Join the blocks into rows. Press the seam allowances in opposite directions from row to row. Join the rows and press the seam allowances in one direction.

FINISHING THE QUILT

For detailed instructions on finishing techniques, refer to "Finishing Your Quilt" on page 77.

1. Cut and piece the backing fabric so it's 3" to 6" larger than the quilt top. Layer the quilt top with batting and backing. Baste the layers together.

2. Hand or machine quilt as desired. See "Quilting Suggestions" below.

3. Square up the quilt sandwich.

4. Use the dark-red 2½"-wide strips to make and attach the binding.

QUILTING SUGGESTIONS

For this modern quilt, I felt it was best to quilt it in a very easy and simple way. Horizontal lines were quilted to disguise the block lines and draw your eye across the quilt top. Using the block seams as a guide, the horizontal lines don't need to be marked, which makes them quick and easy to quilt.

Quilt assembly

AMISH BARS

Amish Bars is a very old and traditional design that still looks striking today. This simple quilt pattern lets you boldly show off your favorite colors and makes the perfect piece of art for a modern home. The wide bands of color also make the perfect place to showcase traditional Amish quilting designs.

- **FINISHED QUILT**
  64½" x 64½"

AMISH TO URBAN
See "Horizon Lines" on page 23 for an urban twist on this Amish quilt.

MATERIALS

Yardage is based on 42"-wide fabric.

1⅞ yards of navy solid for bars, border squares, and binding
1½ yards of plum solid for outer border
1½ yards of medium-green solid for inner border
1⅓ yards of light-green solid for bars
4 yards of fabric for backing
69" x 69" piece of batting

CUTTING

From the *lengthwise* grain of the navy solid, cut:
4 squares, 8½" x 8½"
4 strips, 6½" x 42½"

From the *crosswise* grain of the remaining navy solid, cut:
7 strips, 2½" x 42"

From the *lengthwise* grain of the light-green solid, cut:
3 strips, 6½" x 42½"

From the *lengthwise* grain of the medium-green solid, cut:
2 strips, 3½" x 48½"
2 strips, 3½" x 42½"

From the *lengthwise* grain of the plum solid, cut:
4 strips, 8½" x 48½"

■ "Amish Bars," pieced by Myra Harder and quilted by Katie Friesen

ASSEMBLING THE QUILT TOP

1. Join the navy 6½"-wide strips and light-green strips side by side, alternating the colors as shown. Press the seam allowances toward the navy strips. The quilt center should measure 42½" x 42½".

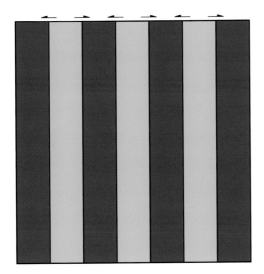

2. Sew the medium-green 42½"-long strips to opposite sides of the quilt center. Press the seam allowances toward the medium-green strips. Sew the medium-green 48½"-long strips to the top and bottom of the quilt top to complete the inner border. Press the seam allowances toward the inner border.

3. Sew plum strips to opposite sides of the quilt top. Press the seam allowances toward the plum strips.

4. Sew a navy square to each end of the remaining plum strips. Press the seam allowances toward the plum strips. Sew the strips to the top and bottom of

the quilt top to complete the outer border. Press the seam allowances toward the outer border.

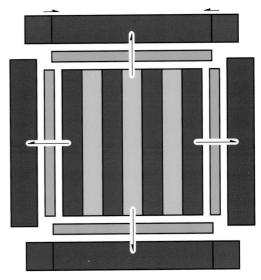

Quilt assembly

FINISHING THE QUILT

For detailed instructions on finishing techniques, refer to "Finishing Your Quilt" on page 77.

1. Cut and piece the backing fabric so it's 3" to 6" larger than the quilt top. Layer the quilt top with batting and backing. Baste the layers together.

2. Hand or machine quilt as desired. See "Quilting Suggestions" below.

3. Square up the quilt sandwich.

4. Use the navy 2½"-wide strips to make and attach the binding.

QUILTING SUGGESTIONS

Following the Amish footsteps, "Amish Bars" was quilted in a very traditional fashion. A diagonal grid was quilted across all of the bars in the quilt center. The inner border has a diamond and seed pattern, and the outer border features a flowing feather pattern.

■ "Horizon Lines," pieced by Myra Harder and quilted by Katie Friesen

HORIZON LINES

The beauty of living on the prairie is that I get to see vast expanses of color spread across our fields during the day and in our skies every evening. I thought it was quite appropriate to use the Rail Fence block to create a quilt that reflects our prairie life, where you will find color spread from one horizon to the other.

- FINISHED QUILT
  72½" x 96½"

- FINISHED BLOCK
  6" x 6"

URBAN TO AMISH

See "Amish Bars" on page 19 for the Amish inspiration for this urban quilt.

MATERIALS

Yardage is based on 42"-wide fabric.

2⅜ yards of white print for sashing
12 strips *each*, 2½" wide, of assorted green, blue, red, yellow, and teal prints for blocks (60 total)
¾ yard of dark-teal print for binding
6 yards of fabric for backing
77" x 101" piece of batting

CUTTING

From the white print, cut:
12 strips, 6½" x 42"

From the dark-teal print, cut:
9 strips, 2½" x 42"

MAKING THE BLOCKS

1. Using the 2½"-wide strips from one color family, join three strips along their long edges as shown to make a strip set. Press the seam allowances in one direction. Make a total of four strip sets. From the strip sets, cut 24 blocks, 6½" wide.

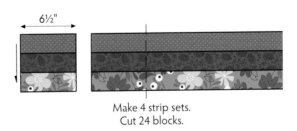

Make 4 strip sets.
Cut 24 blocks.

2. Repeat step 1 to make 24 blocks from each color family (120 blocks total).

ASSEMBLING THE QUILT TOP

1. Using the blocks from one color family, lay out the blocks in two rows of 12 blocks each, rotating every other block 90° as shown. Join the blocks into rows. Press the seam allowances in opposite directions from row to row. Join the rows to complete the section. Press the seam allowances in one direction. The section should measure 12½" x 72½".

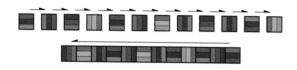

2. Repeat step 1 to make one section from each color family. Make a total of five sections.

3. Join two white strips end to end. Trim the pieced strip to measure 72½" long. Repeat to make a total of six pieced strips.

4. Lay out the five sections and six white strips, alternating them as shown in the quilt assembly diagram below. Join the sections and strips to complete the quilt top. Press the seam allowances in the directions indicated.

FINISHING THE QUILT

For detailed instructions on finishing techniques, refer to "Finishing Your Quilt" on page 77.

1. Cut and piece the backing fabric so it's 3" to 6" larger than the quilt top. Layer the quilt top with batting and backing. Baste the layers together.

2. Hand or machine quilt as desired. See "Quilting Suggestions" below.

3. Square up the quilt sandwich.

4. Use the dark-teal 2½"-wide strips to make and attach the binding.

QUILTING SUGGESTIONS

To add a little texture to the quilt, a diagonal line was quilted from one block to another, forming zigzag lines across the quilt. Between the zigzag lines, Katie quilted vertical lines running across each colored section to add a little drama to the finished quilt.

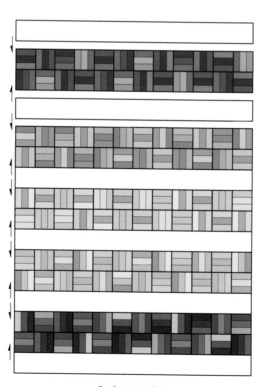

Quilt assembly

AMISH
LOG CABIN

One of the most well-known and recognizable quilt patterns in the world is the Log Cabin. This pattern has reportedly even been found in a 3000-year-old Egyptian tomb. The Log Cabin has been a favorite among quilters for generations. This one simple block can be used to create countless layouts and color combinations. My version has a traditional red center square, which represents the hearth in the center of the home.

- **FINISHED QUILT**
  70½" x 88½"

- **FINISHED BLOCK**
  9" x 9"

AMISH TO URBAN
See "Marrakech" on page 31 for an urban twist on this Amish quilt.

MATERIALS

Yardage is based on 42"-wide fabric.

3¾ yards of navy solid for blocks, inner border, and binding
2⅓ yards of dark-red solid for blocks and outer border
1¼ yards of medium-red solid for blocks
⅔ yard of green solid for blocks
½ yard of teal solid for blocks
5¼ yards of fabric for backing
75" x 93" piece of batting

CUTTING

From the navy solid, cut:
16 strips, 2½" x 42"
53 strips, 1½" x 42"; crosscut into:
    48 rectangles, 1½" x 8½"
    48 rectangles, 1½" x 7½"
    48 rectangles, 1½" x 6½"
    48 rectangles, 1½" x 5½"
    48 rectangles, 1½" x 4½"
    48 rectangles, 1½" x 3½"
    48 rectangles, 1½" x 2½"
    48 squares, 1½" x 1½"

From the medium-red solid, cut:
26 strips, 1½" x 42"; crosscut into:
    48 rectangles, 1½" x 9½"
    48 rectangles, 1½" x 8½"
    48 squares, 1½" x 1½"

From the teal solid, cut:
8 strips, 1½" x 42"; crosscut into:
    48 rectangles, 1½" x 3½"
    48 rectangles, 1½" x 2½"

Continued on page 27

■ "Amish Log Cabin," pieced by Betty Klassen and quilted by Katie Friesen

Continued from page 25

From the green solid, cut:

13 strips, 1½" x 42"; crosscut into:
    48 rectangles, 1½" x 5½"
    48 rectangles, 1½" x 4½"

From the *lengthwise grain* of the dark-red solid, cut:

2 strips, 6½" x 76½"
2 strips, 6½" x 70½"
48 rectangles, 1½" x 7½"
48 rectangles, 1½" x 6½"

MAKING THE BLOCKS

Each block is constructed by sewing rectangles in a counterclockwise direction around a center square. After sewing each seam, press the seam allowances toward the newly added square or rectangle.

1. Sew a navy square to the bottom of a medium-red square. Sew a navy 1½" x 2½" rectangle to the right side of the medium-red square. Make 48 units.

Make 48.

2. Sew a teal 1½" x 2½" rectangle to the top of the medium-red square. Sew a teal 1½" x 3½" rectangle to the left side of the medium-red square to make a center unit. Make 48 units.

Make 48.

3. Sew a navy 1½" x 3½" rectangle to the bottom of a center unit. Sew a navy 1½" x 4½" rectangle to the right side of the unit. Make 48 units.

Make 48.

4. Sew a green 1½" x 4½" rectangle to the top of a unit from step 3. Sew a green 1½" x 5½" rectangle to the left side of the unit. Make 48 units.

Make 48.

5. Sew a navy 1½" x 5½" rectangle to the bottom of a unit from step 4. Sew a navy 1½" x 6½" rectangle to the right side of the unit. Make 48 units.

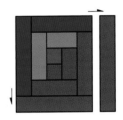

Make 48.

6. Sew a dark-red 1½" x 6½" rectangle to the top of a unit from step 5. Sew a dark-red 1½" x 7½" rectangle to the left side of the block. Make 48 units.

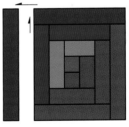

Make 48.

7. Sew a navy 1½" x 7½" rectangle to the bottom of a unit from step 6. Sew a navy 1½" x 8½" rectangle to the right side of the unit. Make 48 units.

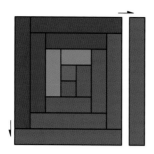

Make 48.

8. Sew a medium-red 1½" x 8½" rectangle to the top of a unit from step 7. Sew a medium-red 1½" x 9½" rectangle to the left side of the unit to complete a block. Make 48 blocks.

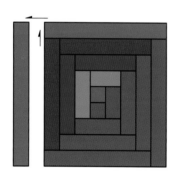

Make 48.

ASSEMBLING THE QUILT TOP

You can assemble Log Cabin blocks in various ways to create many different quilts. It's a great block to play around with and you may prefer an alternate layout. I chose a traditional Barn Raising design.

1. Lay out the blocks in eight rows of six blocks each, rotating the blocks as shown in the quilt assembly diagram on page 29. Join the blocks into rows. Press the seam allowances in opposite directions from row to row. Join the rows and press the seam allowances in one direction. The quilt center should measure 54½" x 72½".

2. Join seven of the navy 2½"-wide strips end to end. From the pieced strip, cut two 72½"-long strips. Sew the strips to opposite sides of the quilt center. Press the seam allowance toward the navy strips.

3. From the remaining pieced strip, cut two 58½"-long strips. Sew the strips to the top and bottom of the quilt top to complete the inner border. Press the seam allowances toward the inner border.

4. Sew the dark-red 76½"-long strips to opposite sides of the quilt top. Press the seam allowances toward the dark-red strips. Sew the dark-red 70½"-long strips to the top and bottom of the quilt top to complete the outer border. Press the seam allowances toward the outer border.

FINISHING THE QUILT

For detailed instructions on finishing techniques, refer to "Finishing Your Quilt" on page 77.

1. Cut and piece the backing fabric so it's 3" to 6" larger than the quilt top. Layer the quilt top with batting and backing. Baste the layers together.

2. Hand or machine quilt as desired. See "Quilting Suggestions," right.

3. Square up the quilt sandwich.

4. Use the remaining navy 2½"-wide strips to make and attach the binding.

QUILTING SUGGESTIONS

Each Log Cabin block was quilted in the ditch along the seam lines. Then, to contrast with the linear quilting, Katie quilted an egg-and-dart design in the inner border and feathers around the outer border.

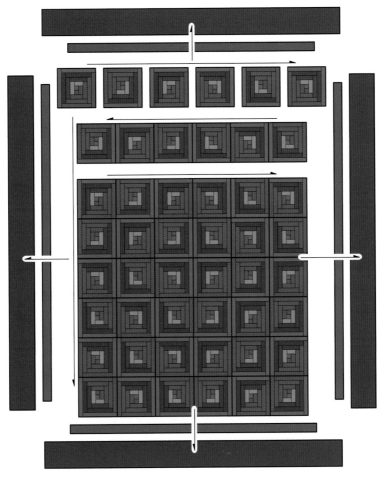

Quilt assembly

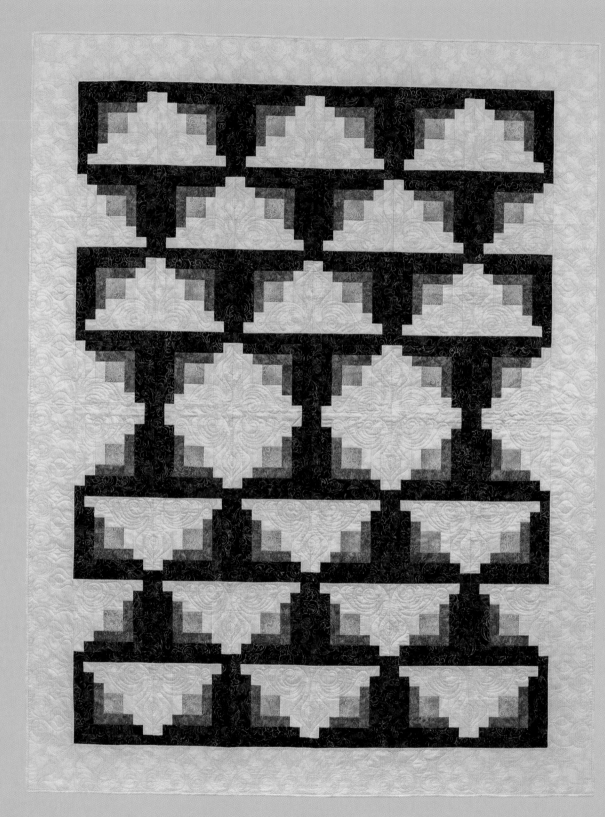

■ "Marrakech," pieced by Myra Harder and quilted by Katie Friesen

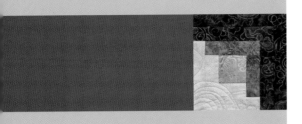

MARRAKECH

There are countless ways to create a quilt with a simple Log Cabin block. When I was playing around with this old favorite, I tried a new layout for the block. I liked the way the blocks formed an outline that feels exotic. I can imagine seeing designs like this on carpets and buildings in a Moroccan bazaar, and it reminds me of one place I hope to visit—Marrakech.

- **FINISHED QUILT**
  86½" x 110½"

- **FINISHED BLOCK**
  12" x 12"

URBAN TO AMISH

See "Amish Log Cabin" on page 25 for the Amish inspiration for this urban quilt.

MATERIALS

Yardage is based on 42"–wide fabric.

6⅝ yards of cream print for blocks, border, and binding
3⅓ yards of deep-purple print for blocks
1 yard of rose print for blocks
⅝ yard of gold print for blocks
7¾ yards of fabric for backing
91" x 115" piece of batting

CUTTING

From the cream print cut:
10 strips, 7½" x 42"
57 strips, 2" x 42"; crosscut into:
    48 rectangles, 2" x 11"
    48 rectangles, 2" x 9½"
    48 rectangles, 2" x 8"
    48 rectangles, 2" x 6½"
    48 rectangles, 2" x 5"
    48 rectangles, 2" x 3½"
11 strips, 2½" x 42"

From the gold print, cut:
5 strips, 3½" x 42"; crosscut into 48 squares, 3½" x 3½"

From the rose print, cut:
14 strips, 2" x 42"; crosscut into:
    48 rectangles, 2" x 6½"
    48 rectangles, 2" x 5"

From the deep-purple print, cut:
54 strips, 2" x 42"; crosscut into:
    48 rectangles, 2" x 12½"
    48 rectangles, 2" x 11"
    48 rectangles, 2" x 9½"
    48 rectangles, 2" x 8"

MAKING THE BLOCKS

Each block is constructed by sewing rectangles in a counterclockwise direction around a center square. After sewing each seam, press the seam allowances toward the just-added rectangle.

1. Sew a cream 2" x 3½" rectangle to the bottom of a gold 3½" square. Sew a cream 2" x 5" rectangle to the right side of the gold square. Make a total of 48 units.

Make 48.

2. Sew a rose 2" x 5" rectangle to the top of a unit from step 1. Sew a rose 2" x 6½" rectangle to the left side of the unit to make a center unit. Make a total of 48 units.

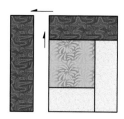

Make 48.

3. Sew a cream 2" x 6½" rectangle to the bottom of a center unit from step 2. Sew a cream 2" x 8" rectangle to the right side of the center unit. Make 48 units.

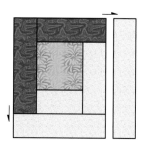

Make 48.

4. Sew a deep-purple 2" x 8" rectangle to the top of a unit from step 3. Sew a deep-purple 2" x 9½" rectangle to the left side of the unit. Make 48 units.

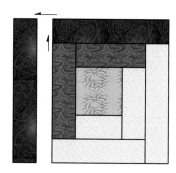

Make 48.

5. Sew a cream 2" x 9½" rectangle to the bottom of a unit from step 4. Sew a cream 2" x 11" rectangle to the right side of the unit. Make 48 units.

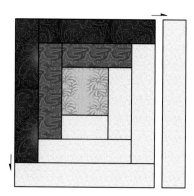

Make 48.

6. Sew a deep-purple 2" x 11" rectangle to the top of a unit from step 5. Sew a deep-purple 2" x 12½" rectangle to the left side of the unit to complete the block. Make a total of 48 blocks.

Make 48.

ASSEMBLING THE QUILT TOP

1. Lay out the blocks in eight rows of six blocks each, rotating the blocks in each row and from row to row as shown in the quilt assembly diagram below. Note that the bottom half of the quilt top is a mirror image of the top half.

2. Join the blocks into rows. Press the seam allowances in opposite directions from row to row. Join the rows and press the seam allowances in one direction. The quilt top should measure 72½" x 96½".

3. Join the cream 7½"-wide strips end to end. From the pieced strip, cut two 96½"-long strips and sew them to opposite sides of the quilt center. Press the seam allowances toward the cream strips.

4. From the remaining pieced strip, cut two 86½"-long strips. Sew the strips to the top and bottom of the quilt top to complete the border. Press the seam allowances toward the border.

FINISHING THE QUILT

For detailed instructions on finishing techniques, refer to "Finishing Your Quilt" on page 77.

1. Cut and piece the backing fabric so it's 3" to 6" larger than the quilt top. Layer the quilt top with batting and backing. Baste the layers together.

2. Hand or machine quilt as desired. See "Quilting Suggestions" below.

3. Square up the quilt sandwich.

4. Use the cream 2½"-wide strips to make and attach the binding.

QUILTING SUGGESTIONS

I wanted to reflect the spirit of Marrakech in the quilting motif. In the blocks, a scrolling design was quilted over the light areas and the seam lines were echo quilted on the dark sides. A similar scrolling design was quilted into the border as well, adding texture to the quilt.

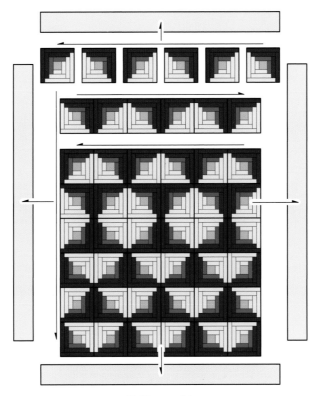

Quilt assembly

■ "Lone Star," pieced by Betty Klassen and quilted by Katie Friesen

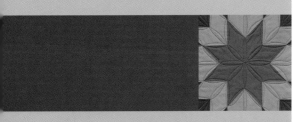

LONE STAR

Quilts using the Lone Star design are always striking, and I have seen them done in many wonderful fabric combinations. However, I personally love the ones that are pieced in strong solid colors. This timeless pattern has been created by Amish women for generations, and is often referred to by another name—Star of Bethlehem. Based on how popular it still is, I'm sure they'll be making it for generations to come.

- **FINISHED QUILT**
  64½" x 64½"

AMISH TO URBAN
See "Urban Ohio" on page 39 for an urban twist on this Amish quilt.

MATERIALS

Yardage is based on 42"-wide fabric.

2 yards of plum solid for center star and border
2 yards of navy solid for setting triangles, setting squares, and binding
⅞ yard of teal solid for center star and corner squares
½ yard of green solid for center star
⅜ yard of light-green solid for center star
¼ yard of light-purple solid for center star
4 yards of fabric for backing
69" x 69" piece of batting

CUTTING

From the *lengthwise* grain of the plum solid, cut:
4 strips, 7½" x 50½"

From the *crosswise* grain of the remaining plum solid, cut:
5 strips, 2½" x 42"

From the teal solid, cut:
8 strips, 2½" x 42"
4 squares, 7½" x 7½"

From the green solid, cut:
6 strips, 2½" x 42"

From the light-green solid, cut:
4 strips, 2½" x 42"

From the light-purple solid, cut:
2 strips, 2½" x 42"

From the navy solid, cut:
2 squares, 16" x 16"; cut the squares in half diagonally to yield
    4 triangles
4 squares, 15⅛" x 15⅛"
7 strips, 2½" x 42"

MAKING THE DIAMOND UNITS

1. Staggering the ends of the strips by 2½", join one plum, one teal, one green, one light-green, and one light-purple 2½"-wide strip along their long edges as shown to make strip-set 1. Press the seam allowances in one direction. Make a total of two units.

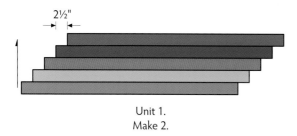

2½"

Unit 1.
Make 2.

2. Using a rotary cutter and a ruler with 45° markings, align the 45° line with the seam line of a strip set as shown. Trim off the irregular ends of the strip set.

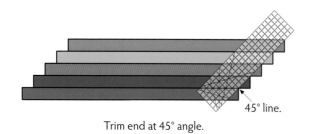

45° line.

Trim end at 45° angle.

3. Rotate the strip set and measure 2½" from the freshly cut end of the strip set; cut a 2½" wide segment. Cut a total of 16 segments.

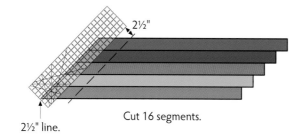

2½"

Cut 16 segments.

2½" line.

4. Repeating steps 1–3, join two teal, one plum, one green, and one light-green strip in the order shown to make strip-set 2. Make two units and cut 16 segments, 2½" wide.

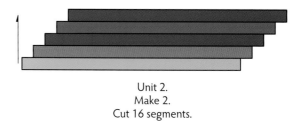

Unit 2.
Make 2.
Cut 16 segments.

5. Repeating steps 1–3, join two green, two teal, and one plum strip in the order shown to make strip-set 3. Cut eight segments, 2½" wide.

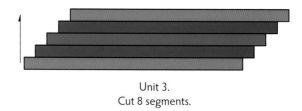

Unit 3.
Cut 8 segments.

6. Lay out two unit 1 segments, two unit 2 segments, and one unit 3 segment as shown, making sure to rotate one of the unit 1 segments and one of the unit 2 segments. Place two segments right sides together and pin to match the seam intersections. The ends of the segments will be offset ¼" as shown. Sew the segments together using a ¼"-wide seam allowance. Pin and sew the remaining segments together in the same way to make a diamond unit. Press the seam allowances in one direction.

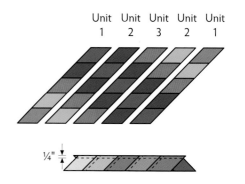

Unit 1 Unit 2 Unit 3 Unit 2 Unit 1

¼"

7. Repeat step 6 to make a total of eight diamond units.

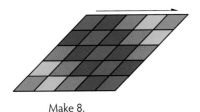

Make 8.

ASSEMBLING THE QUILT TOP

1. Pin two diamond units right sides together, matching the seam intersections. Starting at the diamond tip, sew the seam, stopping ¼" from the inner corner and backstitch. Press the seam allowances in one direction. Make a total of four diamond pairs.

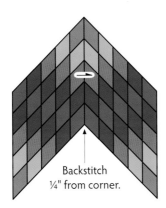

Backstitch
¼" from corner.

2. Sew two diamond pairs together in the same manner to make a half-star unit. Press the seam allowances in one direction. Repeat to make a second half-star unit.

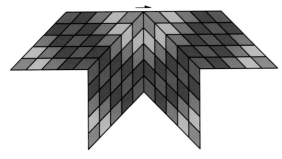

Make 2.

3. With right sides together, align and pin two half-star units together, matching the seam intersections. Sew the center seam, starting and stopping ¼" from each corner with a backstitch. Press the center seam in one direction.

4. Place a navy square on top of a diamond unit, right sides together and raw edges aligned. Sew from the outside edge to the inside corner, stopping ¼" from the edge. With the needle in the down position, pivot and sew the square to the edge of the second diamond unit. Press the seam allowances toward the square. In the same way, sew navy squares to the three remaining corners.

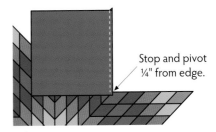

Stop and pivot
¼" from edge.

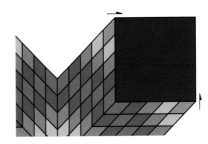

5. Repeat step 4 to sew navy triangles to the sides of the star as shown in the quilt assembly diagram on page 38 to complete the quilt center. The quilt center should measure 50½" x 50½".

6. Sew plum 50½"-long strips to opposite sides of the quilt center. Press the seam allowances toward the plum strips.

7. Sew a teal square to each end of both remaining plum 7½"-wide strips. Press the seam allowances toward the strips. Sew the strips to the top and bottom of the quilt center. Press the seam allowances toward the border.

FINISHING THE QUILT

For detailed instructions on finishing techniques, refer to "Finishing Your Quilt" on page 77.

1. Cut and piece the backing fabric so it's 3" to 6" larger than the quilt top. Layer the quilt top with batting and backing. Baste the layers together.

2. Hand or machine quilt as desired. See "Quilting Suggestions" below.

3. Square up the quilt sandwich.

4. Use the navy 2½"-wide strips to make and attach the binding.

QUILTING SUGGESTIONS

In keeping with the traditional quilting found on a Lone Star pattern, an arching melon design was quilted over each diamond. A traditional crosshatch was quilted in the navy squares and triangles. Finally, a beautiful feather design was quilted in the border.

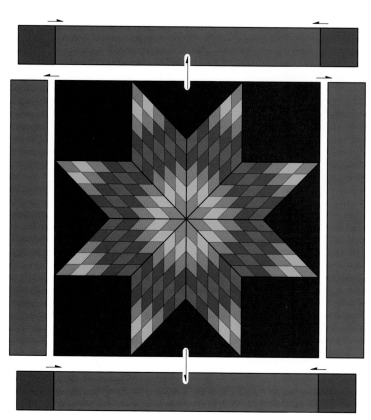

Quilt assembly

URBAN OHIO

I love taking a simple block and making it big! Ohio Star is the perfect block for a modern quilt. To add some interest to the large pieces, I used brightly colored 2½"-wide strips. The final result is a big, bold block that will brighten any room.

- **FINISHED QUILT**
  70½" x 90½"

- **FINISHED BLOCK**
  48" x 48"

URBAN TO AMISH

See "Lone Star" on page 35 for the Amish inspiration for this urban quilt.

MATERIALS

Yardage is based on 42"-wide fabrics.

3¾ yards of white print for block and inner border
2⅛ yards of green print for outer border and binding
1¼ yards *total* of assorted blue, yellow, and green prints for block
5½ yards of fabric for backing
75" x 95" piece of batting
Template plastic, at least 9" x 18"

CUTTING

From the assorted blue, yellow, and green prints, cut a *total* of:
12 strips, 2½" x 42" (For greater variety, cut 14 strips.)

From the white print cut:
5 strips, 16½" x 42"; crosscut *2 of the strips* into 4 squares,
      16½" x 16½"
3 strips, 6½" x 42"
2 squares, 17¼" x 17¼"; cut the squares into quarters diagonally
      to yield 8 triangles

From the green print, cut:
8 strips, 5½" x 42"
9 strips, 2½" x 42"

■ "Urban Ohio," pieced by Myra Harder and quilted by Katie Friesen

MAKING THE OHIO STAR BLOCK

1. Staggering the ends of the strips by 2½", randomly sew four assorted strips together along their long edges to make a strip set. Press the seam allowances in one direction. Make three strip sets. **Note:** For greater variety, as in the quilt shown, make four strip sets.

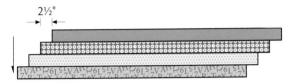

Make 3.

2. Use the triangle pattern on page 43 to make a plastic template. Using the triangle template, cut four triangles from each strip set (12 total).

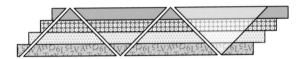

3. Join four triangles from step 2 to make the center unit. Press the seam allowances as indicated. The unit should measure 16½" x 16½".

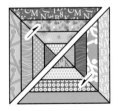
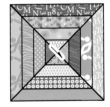

4. Join two triangles from step 2 and two white triangles as shown to make an hourglass unit. Press the seam allowances as indicated. The unit should measure 16½" x 16½". Make four of these units.

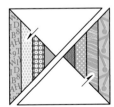
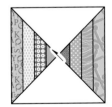

Make 4.

5. Lay out the center unit, four hourglass units, and the four white 16½" squares in three rows as shown. Join the pieces into rows. Press the seam allowances in the directions indicated. Join the rows and press the seam allowances toward the center. The block should measure 48½" x 48½".

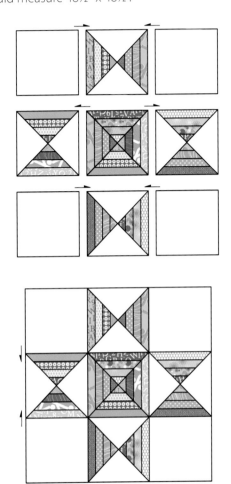

ASSEMBLING THE QUILT TOP

1. Join the white 6½"-wide strips end to end. From the pieced strip, cut two 48½"-long strips and sew them to opposite sides of the star block. Press the seam allowances toward the white border.

2. Join the three white 16½"-wide strips end to end. From the pieced strip, cut two 60½"-long strips and sew them to the top and bottom of the star block to complete the inner border. Press the seam allowances toward the inner border.

3. Join the green 5½"-wide strips end to end. From the pieced strip, cut two 80½"-long strips and sew them to opposite sides of the quilt top. Press the seam allowances toward the green strips.

4. From the remaining pieced strip, cut two 70½"-long strips. Sew the strips to the top and bottom of the quilt top to complete the outer border. Press the seam allowances toward the outer border.

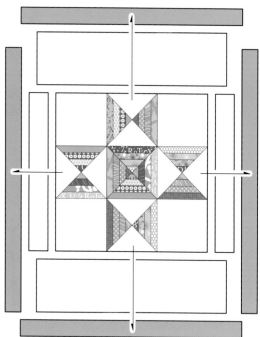

Quilt assembly

FINISHING THE QUILT

For detailed instructions on finishing techniques, refer to "Finishing Your Quilt" on page 77.

1. Cut and piece the backing fabric so it's 3" to 6" larger than the quilt top. Layer the quilt top with batting and backing. Baste the layers together.

2. Hand or machine quilt as desired. See "Quilting Suggestions" below.

3. Square up the quilt sandwich.

4. Use the green 2½"-wide strips to make and attach the binding.

QUILTING SUGGESTIONS

The background area of this quilt is a great place to show off a gorgeous quilting design. Katie and I worked together to come up with a plan to echo the star by quilting straight lines to create a narrow frame. The rest of the open area was filled with airy swirls that would make the star stand out and shine.

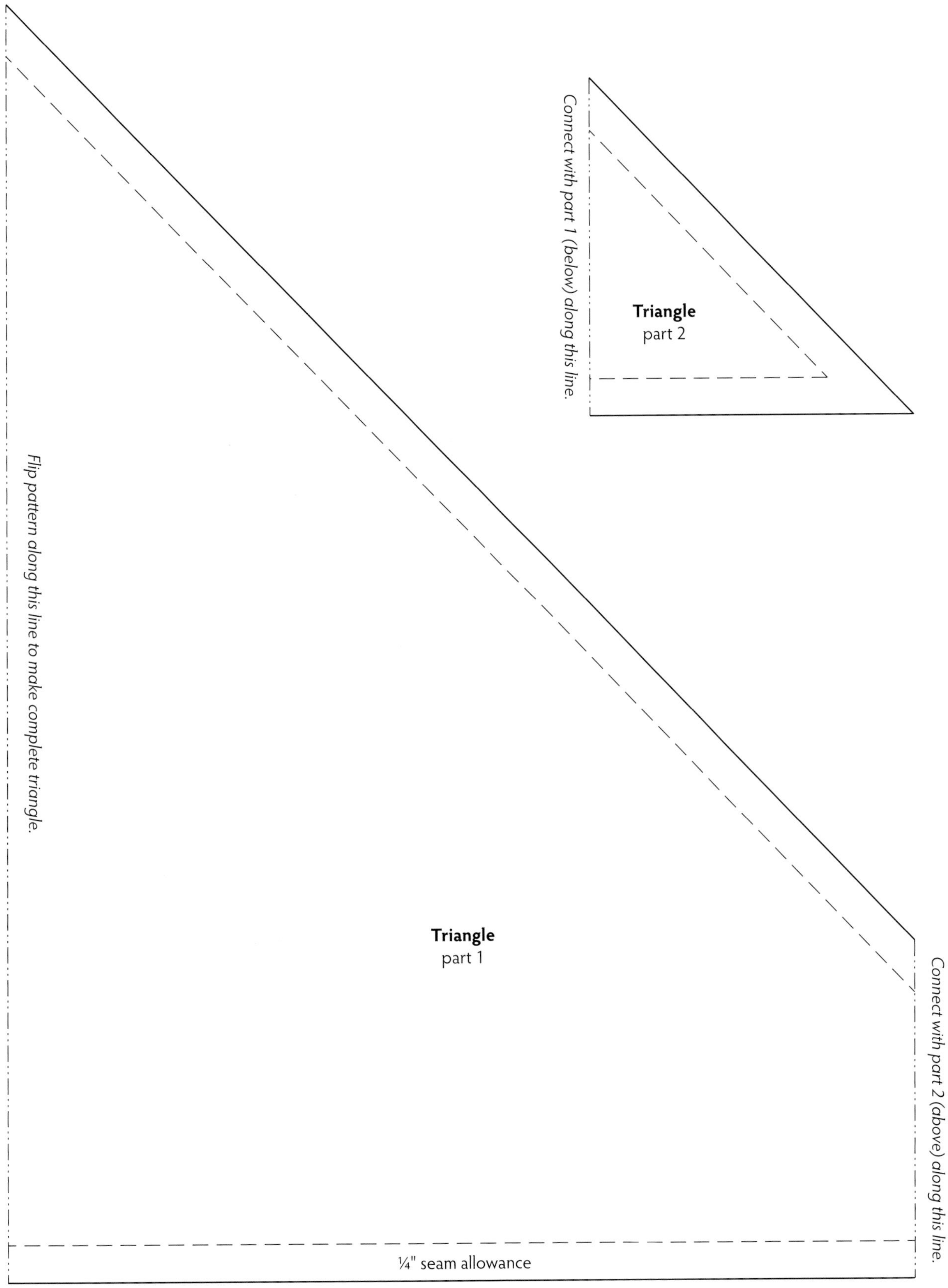

Triangle
part 2

Connect with part 1 (below) along this line.

Triangle
part 1

Flip pattern along this line to make complete triangle.

Connect with part 2 (above) along this line.

¼" seam allowance

■ "Ocean Waves," pieced by Myra Harder and quilted by Katie Friesen

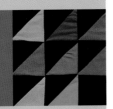

OCEAN WAVES

Ocean Waves is a classic pattern that's been around for generations. I think it's the motion created by the piecing that makes it so appealing. Even though Amish communities are mostly landlocked, their quilters could also appreciate the beauty of the sea.

- **FINISHED QUILT**
  71½" x 71½"

- **FINISHED BLOCK**
  12" x 12"

AMISH TO URBAN

See "South Pacific" on page 49 for an urban twist on this Amish quilt.

MATERIALS

Yardage is based on 42"-wide fabric.

5 yards of black solid for blocks, outer border, and binding
¼ yard *each* of 12 assorted purple, blue, and green solids for blocks
⅝ yard of purple solid for inner border
4⅜ yards of fabric for backing
76" x 76" piece of batting

CUTTING

From the *lengthwise* grain of the black solid, cut:
2 strips, 9½" x 71½"
2 strips, 9½" x 53½"

From the *crosswise* grain of the remaining black solid, cut:
12 strips, 4" x 42"
6 strips, 3½" x 42"; crosscut into 64 squares, 3½" x 3½"
8 strips, 2½" x 42"

From *each* of the assorted purple, blue, and green solids, cut:
1 strip, 4" x 42" (12 total)

From the purple solid, cut:
6 strips, 3" x 42"

MAKING THE BLOCKS

1. On the wrong side of a purple 4" strip, draw eight vertical lines 4" apart to make eight squares. Draw a diagonal line across each square as shown.

Mark lines.

2. Layer a marked strip from step 1 right sides together with a black 4"-wide strip. Stitch ¼" on each side of the marked lines. Cut the squares apart on the drawn lines to make 16 half-square-triangle units. Press the seam allowances toward the black triangles. Trim each unit to measure 3½" x 3½".

3½"

3½"

Make 16.

3. Repeat steps 1 and 2 using the remaining purple, blue, green, and black 4" strips to make 176 half-square-triangle units. You'll have a total of 192 units.

4. Using one half-square-triangle unit from each solid color, lay out 12 half-square-triangle units and four black 3½" squares in four rows as shown. Sew the pieces together into rows. Press the seam allowances in opposite directions from row to row. Join the rows to complete the block. Press the seam allowances in one direction. Make a total of 16 blocks.

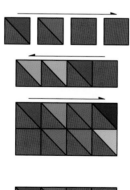

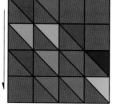

Make 16.

COLOR PLACEMENT

I used the same half-square-triangle color (dark purple) in the upper-left corner of each block to create a pinwheel in the center of the quilt. I used the same half-square-triangle color (light purple) in the lower-right corner of each block to create four pinwheels in the quilt.

ASSEMBLING THE QUILT TOP

1. Lay out the blocks in four rows of four blocks each, rotating the blocks to form a pinwheel where four blocks meet as shown in the quilt assembly diagram on page 47.

2. Join the blocks into rows. Press the seam allowances in opposite directions from row to row. Join the rows and press the seam allowances in one direction. The quilt top should measure 48½" x 48½".

3. Join the purple 3"-wide strips end to end. From the pieced strip, cut two 48½"-long strips and sew them to opposite sides of the quilt center. Press the seam allowances toward the light-purple strips.

4. From the remaining pieced strip, cut two 53½"-long strips. Sew the strips to the top and bottom of the quilt top to complete the inner border. Press the seam allowances toward the inner border.

5. Sew the black 53½"-long strips to opposite sides of the quilt top. Press the seam allowances toward the black strips. Sew the black 71½"-long strips to the top and bottom of the quilt top. Press the seam allowances toward the outer border.

FINISHING THE QUILT

For detailed instructions on finishing techniques, refer to "Finishing Your Quilt" on page 77.

1. Cut and piece the backing fabric so it's 3" to 6" larger than the quilt top. Layer the quilt top with batting and backing. Baste the layers together.

2. Hand or machine quilt as desired. See "Quilting Suggestions," right.

3. Square up the quilt sandwich.

4. Use the black 2½"-wide strips to make and attach the binding.

QUILTING SUGGESTIONS

The quilting designs on traditional Ocean Waves quilts are very similar to the "South Pacific" quilt on page 49. A feather design was quilted in the background areas and simple lines were quilted in the wide outer border.

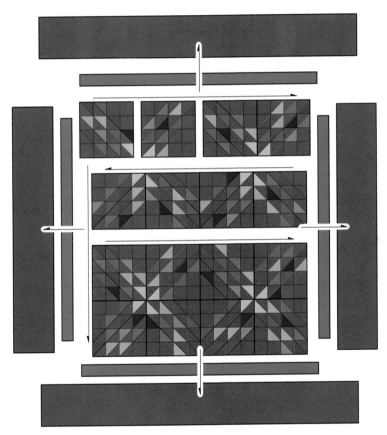

Quilt assembly

■ "South Pacific," pieced by Myra Harder and quilted by Katie Friesen

SOUTH PACIFIC

The traditional Ocean Waves quilt pattern has been admired and collected for hundreds of years. I love the look of this design, but I wanted to make it more fun, with considerably fewer triangles. Increasing the block size and working with several packs of charm squares gave this quilt a cheerful, laid-back feeling. And who wouldn't like to be relaxing in the South Pacific?

- **FINISHED QUILT**
  88½" x 96½"

- **FINISHED BLOCK**
  16" x 16"

URBAN TO AMISH

See "Ocean Waves" on page 45 for the Amish inspiration for this urban quilt.

MATERIALS

Yardage is based on 42"-wide fabric.

7⅜ yards of ivory print for blocks, border, and binding
⅜ yard *each* of 12 assorted prints for blocks*
8 yards of fabric for backing
93" x 101" piece of batting

*For a scrappy quilt, use 144 charm squares, each at least 5" x 5".

CUTTING

From the *lengthwise* grain of the ivory print, cut:
2 strips, 12½" x 96½"
5 strips, 2½" x 76"

From the *crosswise* grain of the remaining ivory print, cut:
18 strips, 4⅞" x 42"; crosscut into 144 squares, 4⅞" x 4⅞"
12 strips, 4½" x 42"; crosscut into 96 squares, 4½" x 4½"

From *each* of the assorted prints cut:
2 strips, 4⅞" x 42"; crosscut into 12 squares, 4⅞" x 4⅞" (144 total)

MAKING THE BLOCKS

1. Draw a diagonal line on the wrong side of each ivory 4⅞" square. Layer a marked square right sides together with a print square. Stitch ¼" on each side of the marked line. Cut the squares apart on the drawn line to make two half-square-triangle units. Press the seam allowances toward the print triangle. Make a total of 288 units.

Make 288.

2. Using one half-square-triangle unit from each print, lay out 12 units and four ivory 4½" squares in four rows as shown. Sew the pieces together into rows. Press the seam allowances in opposite directions from row to row. Join the rows to complete the block. Press the seam allowances in one direction. Make a total of 24 blocks.

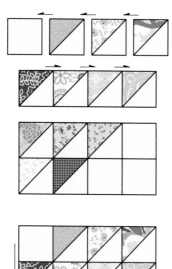

Make 24.

ASSEMBLING THE QUILT TOP

1. Lay out the blocks in six rows of four blocks each, rotating the blocks to form a pinwheel where four blocks meet as shown in the quilt assembly diagram, above right.

2. Join the blocks into rows. Press the seam allowances in opposite directions from row to row. Join the rows and press the seam allowances in one direction. The quilt top should measure 88½" x 96½".

3. Sew the ivory 96½"-long strips to opposite sides of the quilt top. Press the seam allowances toward the ivory strips.

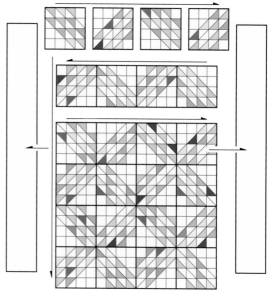

Quilt assembly

FINISHING THE QUILT

For detailed instructions on finishing techniques, refer to "Finishing Your Quilt" on page 77.

1. Cut and piece the backing fabric so it's 3" to 6" larger than the quilt top. Layer the quilt top with batting and backing. Baste the layers together.

2. Hand or machine quilt as desired. See "Quilting Suggestions" below.

3. Square up the quilt sandwich.

4. Use the ivory 2½"-wide strips to make and attach the binding.

QUILTING SUGGESTIONS

Katie created a unique feather to fill the center area of the light background and another original feather to scroll down the sides of the quilt. You could quilt a little swirl in each printed triangle, but Katie left them unquilted. I think the quilting brings a bit of elegance to this classic quilt.

TRIP AROUND THE WORLD

Many of us dream about taking a trip around the world, but in the Amish communities, you'll find they stay much closer to home. (In fact, the pattern we call Trip around the World, they actually refer to as Sunshine and Shadow.) The Amish do travel and visit family around the country, but you'll most often find them working and volunteering around their own towns. The Amish feel it's important to help your neighbors.

■ **FINISHED QUILT**
   60½" x 72½"

AMISH TO URBAN
See "Trip to New York" on page 55 for an urban twist on this Amish quilt.

MATERIALS

Yardage is based on 42"-wide fabric.

2⅞ yards of navy solid for quilt center, outer border, and binding
⅓ yard *each* of 7 assorted solids (teal, light green, medium green, dark green, medium red, dark red, and dark purple) for quilt center
¾ yard of blue solid for quilt center and inner border
3⅔ yards of fabric for backing
65" x 77" piece of batting

CUTTING

From the *lengthwise* grain of the navy solid, cut:
4 strips, 6½" x 60½"

From the *crosswise* grain of the remaining navy solid, cut:
3 strips, 3½" x 42"
7 strips, 2½" x 42"

From the blue solid, cut:
6 strips, 2" x 42"
3 strips, 3½" x 42"

From *each* of the assorted solids, cut:
3 strips, 3½" x 42" (21 total)

■ **"Trip around the World," pieced by Myra Harder and quilted by Katie Friesen**

MAKING THE BLOCKS

Instead of piecing individual squares, it's easier and faster to make this quilt using strip piecing. After cutting segments from the strip sets, you'll need to rearrange some of the squares so that the colors step up or down diagonally across the block.

1. Sew one 3½"-wide strip of each color together along their long edges as shown to make a strip set. Press the seam allowances in one direction. Make a total of three strip sets. Cut the strip sets into 32 segments, 3½" wide.

Make 3 strip sets.
Cut 32 segments.

2. To make block A, lay out seven segments from step 1. Starting on the *left,* keep the first segment as is. On the second segment, remove the stitching between the dark-red square and the purple square at the top of the segment. Sew the dark-red square to the medium-red square at the bottom of the segment. Press the seam allowances toward the top of the segment.

3. On the third segment, remove the stitching between the purple square and the navy square to make a two-square section. Sew the dark-red square to the medium-red square at the bottom of the segment. Press the seam allowances toward the top of the segment.

4. On the fourth segment, remove the stitching between the navy square and the blue square to make a three-square section. Sew the dark-red square to the medium-red square at the bottom of the segment. Press the seam allowances toward the top of the segment. Repeat the process for the remaining three segments.

5. Join the segments to complete the block. Press the seam allowances in one direction. Make a total of two A blocks.

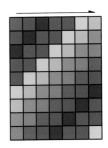

Block A.
Make 2.

6. To make block B, lay out seven segments from step 1. Starting on the *right,* repeat steps 2–5 to make two B blocks as shown. You'll have four segments leftover to use for assembling the quilt top.

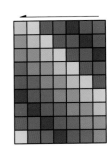

Block B.
Make 2.

ASSEMBLING THE QUILT TOP

1. On two of the remaining segments, remove the stitching between the dark-green square and the medium-green square to make a two-square section. Sew the dark-red square to the medium-red square at the bottom of the segment. Press the seam allowances toward the top of the segment.

2. On one remaining segment, remove the stitching between the dark-green square and the medium-red square. Discard the medium-red square. On the last segment, remove the stitching between the dark-green square and the medium-green square. Discard the two-square section.

3. Lay out the A and B blocks with the segments from steps 1 and 2 as shown. Join the pieces into rows. Press the seam allowances in the directions indicated. Join the rows and press the seam allowances toward the center. The quilt top should measure 45½" x 57½".

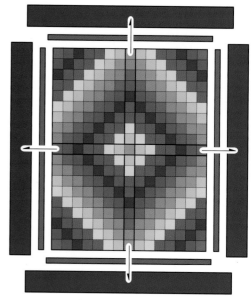

Quilt assembly

FINISHING THE QUILT

For detailed instructions on finishing techniques, refer to "Finishing Your Quilt" on page 77.

1. Cut and piece the backing fabric so it's 3" to 6" larger than the quilt top. Layer the quilt top with batting and backing. Baste the layers together.

2. Hand or machine quilt as desired. See "Quilting Suggestions" below.

3. Square up the quilt sandwich.

4. Use the navy 2½"-wide strips to make and attach the binding.

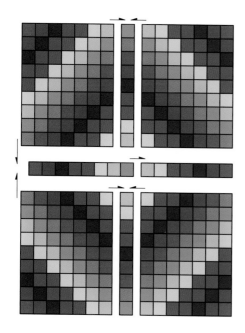

4. Join the blue 2"-wide strips end to end. From the pieced strip, cut two 57½"-long strips and sew them to opposite sides of the quilt center as shown in the quilt assembly diagram, above right. Press the seam allowances toward the blue strips.

5. From the remaining pieced strip, cut two 48½"-long strips. Sew the strips to the top and bottom of the quilt top to complete the inner border. Press the seam allowances toward the inner border.

6. Sew navy 60½"-long strips to opposite sides of the quilt top. Press the seam allowances toward the navy strips. Sew navy 60½"-long strips to the top and bottom of the quilt top to complete the outer border. Press the seam allowances toward the outer border.

QUILTING SUGGESTIONS

To emphasize the colors in the quilt and tie them all together, straight lines were quilted through each round or color. A new version of an old Amish fan design was quilted in the outer border. It reflects how this quilt would have traditionally been quilted by a group of Amish women.

TRIP TO NEW YORK

This modern lap quilt was inspired by my very first trip to New York City when I was a child. Our home in Lancaster was only a few hours away from New York, so my family would make trips into the city. The quilt's buildings are not meant to be mirror images of each other; rather they're my impression of being at Battery Park and seeing Manhattan on one side of the Hudson River and Hoboken, New Jersey, on the other side. It was a whole new landscape for a nine-year-old prairie girl.

- ■ FINISHED QUILT
  50½" x 71½"

URBAN TO AMISH
See "Trip around the World" on page 51 for the Amish inspiration for this urban quilt.

MATERIALS
Yardage is based on 42"-wide fabric.

2½ yards of cream print for quilt center and outer border
15 strips, 2½" wide, of assorted prints for quilt center
¼ yard of black stripe for inner border
⅝ yard of gray print for binding
3¼ yards of fabric for backing
55" x 76" piece of batting

CUTTING

From the cream print, cut:
6 strips, 6½" x 42"
1 strip, 3½" x 36½"
14 strips, 2½" x 42"; crosscut into:
    9 rectangles, 2½" x 24½"
    10 rectangles, 2½" x 21½"
    6 rectangles, 2½" x 18½"
    6 rectangles, 2½" x 15½"
    4 rectangles, 2½" x 12½"
    1 rectangle, 2½" x 6½"

From the assorted strips, cut a *total* of:
1 rectangle, 2½" x 21½"
4 rectangles, 2½" x 15½"
6 rectangles, 2½" x 12½"
6 rectangles, 2½" x 9½"
10 rectangles, 2½" x 6½"
9 rectangles, 2½" x 3½"

From the black stripe, cut:
3 strips, 1½" x 42"
2 strips, 1½" x 38½"

From the gray print, cut:
7 strips, 2½" x 42"

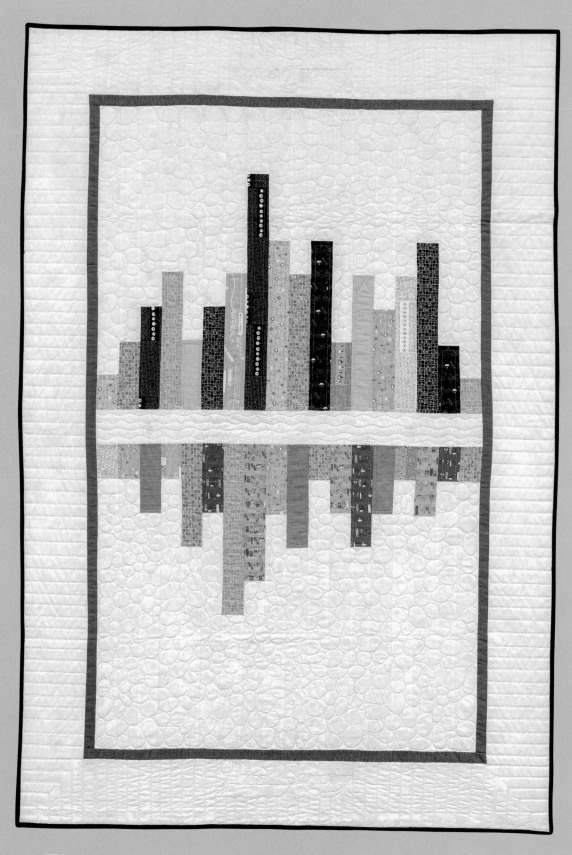

■ "Trip to New York," pieced by Myra Harder and quilted by Katie Friesen

ASSEMBLING THE QUILT TOP

1. Referring to the diagram after step 2, sew print rectangles to cream rectangles to make 27½"-long strips. Press the seam allowances toward the print rectangles. Make a total of 18 strips.

2. Join the strips along their long edges to make the top section of the quilt top. Press the seam allowances in one direction. The section should measure 36½" x 27½".

3. Repeat steps 1 and 2 to make the bottom section of the quilt top.

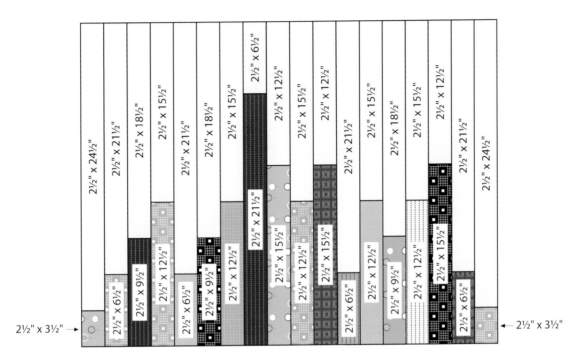

Top section

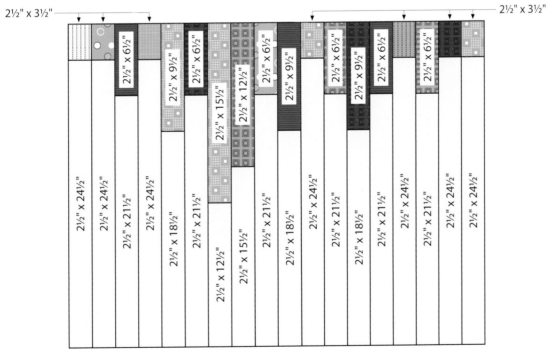

Bottom section

4. Sew the cream 3½" x 36½" strip to the bottom of the top section. Press the seam allowances toward the cream strip. Sew the bottom section to the other side of the cream strip as shown in the quilt assembly diagram below. Press the seam allowances toward the cream strip.

5. Join the black-striped 42"-long strips end to end. From the pieced strip, cut two 57½"-long strips and sew them to opposite sides of the quilt center. Press the seam allowances toward the black-striped strips.

6. Sew the black-striped 38½"-long strips to the top and bottom of the quilt top to complete the inner border. Press the seam allowances toward the inner border.

7. Join the cream 6½"-wide strips end to end. From the pieced strip, cut two 59½"-long strips and sew them to opposite sides of the quilt center. Press the seam allowances toward the inner border.

8. From the remaining pieced strip, cut two 50½"-long strips. Sew the strips to the top and bottom of the quilt top to complete the outer border. Press the seam allowances toward the inner border.

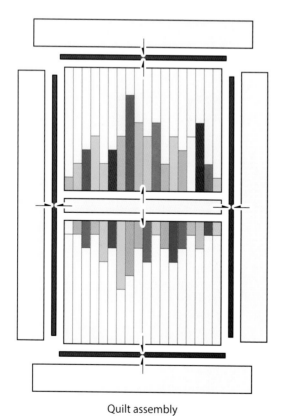

Quilt assembly

FINISHING THE QUILT

For detailed instructions on finishing techniques, refer to "Finishing Your Quilt" on page 77.

1. Cut and piece the backing fabric so it's 3" to 6" larger than the quilt top. Layer the quilt top with batting and backing. Baste the layers together.

2. Hand or machine quilt as desired. See "Quilting Suggestions" below.

3. Square up the quilt sandwich.

4. Use the gray 2½"-wide strips to make and attach the binding.

QUILTING SUGGESTIONS

Katie and I had fun coming up with a quilting plan for this project. To help hide all of the seams in the center of the quilt, Katie quilted round circles in the sky above the buildings. It reminds me of the bright lights of the city that are always shining. Small waves quilted in the cream strip represent the Hudson river. Lines similar to piano keys were quilted in the outer border. However, the best quilting detail came from a friend who asked if it was possible to add names to the quilt. We thought it was a great idea, so *New York* was quilted in the top outer border, and *New Jersey* was quilted in the bottom outer border.

AMISH CENTER DIAMOND

The Center Diamond is a very recognizable Amish design. However, this quilt will always hold special memories for me. When it was time for my family to return to Canada, the Amish women gave my mother an Amish Center Diamond wall hanging as a gift. That very special gift hung in our home for the rest of my childhood.

- **FINISHED QUILT**
  51½" x 51½"

AMISH TO URBAN

See "Lightning Strike" on page 63 for an urban twist on this Amish quilt.

MATERIALS

Yardage is based on 42"-wide fabric.

1½ yards of navy solid for outer border and corner squares
⅔ yard of green solid for quilt center and inner border
½ yard of red solid for center square and corner squares
½ yard of purple solid for setting triangles
3¼ yards of fabric for backing
56" x 56" piece of batting

CUTTING

From the red solid, cut:
1 square, 16½" x 16½"
4 squares, 7½" x 7½"
4 squares, 3½" x 3½"

From the green solid, cut:
4 strips, 3½" x 16½"
4 strips, 3½" x 30½"

From the navy solid, cut:
4 strips, 7½" x 37½"
4 squares, 3½" x 3½"
6 strips, 2½" x 42"

From the purple solid, cut:
2 squares, 16½" x 16½"; cut the squares in half diagonally to yield 4 triangles

"Amish Center Diamond," pieced by Myra Harder and quilted by Katie Friesen

ASSEMBLING THE QUILT TOP

1. Sew green 3½" x 16½" strips to opposite sides of the red 16½" square. Press the seam allowances toward the green strips.

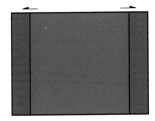

2. Sew a navy 3½" square to each end of the two remaining green 3½" x 16½" strips. Press the seam allowances toward the green strips. Sew these strips to the top and bottom of the red square to complete the center square. Press the seam allowances toward the green strips.

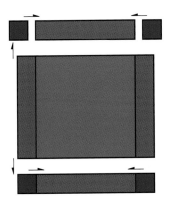

3. Center and sew purple triangles to opposite sides of the center square. Press the seam allowances toward the triangles. Center and sew purple triangles to the remaining two sides of the center square. Press the seam allowances toward the triangles. Trim and square up the quilt center,

making sure to leave ¼" beyond the points of the navy squares for seam allowances.

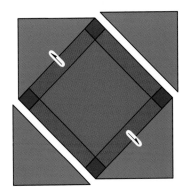

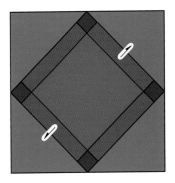

4. Sew green 30½"-long strips to opposite side of the quilt center. Press the seam allowances toward the green strips. Sew a red 3½" square to each end of the two remaining green 30½"-long strips. Press the seam allowances toward the green strips. Sew these strips to the top and bottom of the quilt center to complete the inner border. Press the seam allowances toward the inner border.

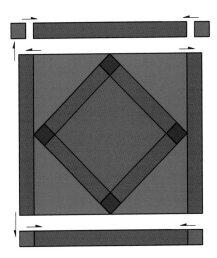

5. Sew navy 7½"-wide strips to opposite sides of the quilt top. Press the seam allowances toward the navy strips. Sew a red 7½" square to each end of the two remaining navy 7½"-wide strips. Press the seam allowances toward the navy strips. Sew these strips to the top and bottom of the quilt center to complete the outer border. Press the seam allowances toward the outer border.

FINISHING THE QUILT

For detailed instructions on finishing techniques, refer to "Finishing Your Quilt" on page 77.

1. Cut and piece the backing fabric so it's 3" to 6" larger than the quilt top. Layer the quilt top with batting and backing. Baste the layers together.

2. Hand or machine quilt as desired. See "Quilting Suggestions" below.

3. Square up the quilt sandwich.

4. Use the navy 2½"-wide strips to make and attach the binding.

QUILTING SUGGESTIONS

This quilt was quilted with a traditional Amish quilting design. A feathered wreath design was quilted in the center of the red square. The purple triangles feature diagonal crosshatching. Small designs and feathers were quilted in the borders.

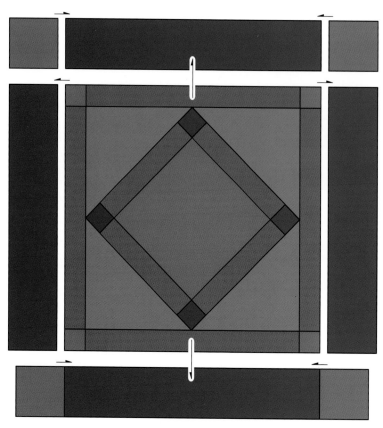

Quilt assembly

LIGHTNING STRIKE

This quilt came together by surprise and the more I worked on it, the more I loved it. This quilt is based on a traditional Center Diamond design. However, when I removed the borders from the center diamond, I was left with a Monkey Wrench block. With careful color placement, this quilt is very striking.

- **FINISHED QUILT**
  78½" x 90½"

- **FINISHED BLOCK**
  12" x 12"

URBAN TO AMISH

See "Amish Center Diamond" on page 59 for the Amish inspiration for this urban quilt.

MATERIALS

Yardage is based on 42"-wide fabric.

5⅛ yards of white print for blocks and border
2¼ yards of green print for blocks
1⅛ yards of red print for blocks and binding
⅞ yard of gray print for blocks
7 yards of fabric for backing
83" x 95" piece of batting

CUTTING

From the *lengthwise* grain of the white print, cut:
2 strips, 9½" x 78½"
2 strips, 9½" x 72½"

From the *crosswise* grain of the remaining white print, cut:
6 strips, 7" x 42"; crosscut into 30 squares, 7" x 7". Cut the squares in half diagonally to yield 60 triangles.
5 strips, 5¼" x 42"; crosscut into 30 squares, 5¼" x 5¼". Cut the squares in half diagonally to yield 60 triangles.
3 strips, 4" x 42"; crosscut into 30 squares, 4" x 4". Cut the squares in half diagonally to yield 60 triangles.
3 strips, 3" x 42"; crosscut into 30 squares, 3" x 3". Cut the squares in half diagonally to yield 60 triangles.

From the red print, cut:
3 strips, 3½" x 42"; crosscut into 30 squares, 3½" x 3½"
9 strips, 2½" x 42"

From the green print, cut:
5 strips, 7" x 42"; crosscut into 24 squares, 7" x 7". Cut the squares in half diagonally to yield 48 triangles.
4 strips, 5¼" x 42"; crosscut into 24 squares, 5¼" x 5¼". Cut the squares in half diagonally to yield 48 triangles.
3 strips, 4" x 42"; crosscut into 24 squares, 4" x 4". Cut the squares in half diagonally to yield 48 triangles.
2 strips, 3" x 42"; crosscut into 24 squares, 3" x 3". Cut the squares in half diagonally to yield 48 triangles.

Continued on page 65

■ "Lightning Strike," pieced by Myra Harder and quilted by Katie Friesen

Continued from page 63

From the gray print, cut:

2 strips, 7" x 42"; crosscut into 6 squares, 7" x 7". Cut the squares in half diagonally to yield 12 triangles.

1 strip, 5¼" x 42"; crosscut into 6 squares, 5¼" x 5¼". Cut the squares in half diagonally to yield 12 triangles.

1 strip, 4" x 42"; crosscut into 6 squares, 4" x 4". Cut the squares in half diagonally to yield 12 triangles.

1 strip, 3" x 42"; crosscut into 6 squares, 3" x 3". Cut the squares in half diagonally to yield 12 triangles.

MAKING THE BLOCKS

Each block is constructed by sewing triangles in a counterclockwise direction around a center square. After sewing each seam, press the seam allowances toward the newly added triangle.

1. Sew a green 3" triangle to the top of a red square. Sew another green 3" triangle to the left side of the red square. Sew a white 3" triangle to the bottom of the red square. Sew another white 3" triangle to the right side of the red square to complete the center unit. The unit should measure 4¾" x 4¾". Make 24 units.

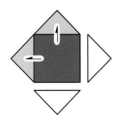 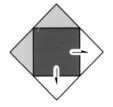

Make 24.

2. Sew white 4" triangles to the upper-right and upper-left corners of each center unit. Sew green 4" triangles to the lower-right and lower-left corners of each unit. Trim each unit to measure 6½" x 6½",

making sure to leave ¼" beyond all points for seam allowances. Make 24 units.

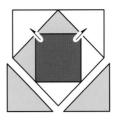

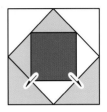

Make 24.

3. Sew white 5¼" triangles to the top and left sides of each unit. Sew green 5¼" triangles to the bottom and right sides of each unit. Trim each unit to measure 9" x 9". Make 24 units.

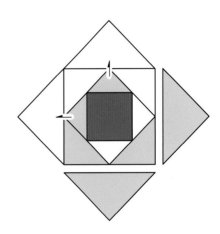

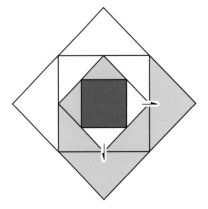

Make 24.

4. Sew green 7" triangles to the upper-right and upper-left corners of each unit. Sew white 7" triangles to the lower-right and lower-left corners of each unit to complete the blocks. Trim each block to measure 12½" x 12½". Make 24 green blocks.

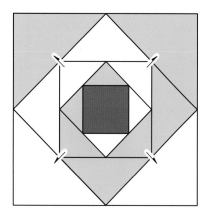

Make 24.

5. Repeat steps 1–4 using the gray triangles, white triangles, and remaining red squares to make six gray blocks.

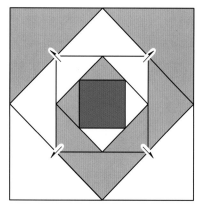

Make 6.

ASSEMBLING THE QUILT TOP

I found it easiest to assemble this quilt in vertical columns.

1. Lay out the blocks in five rows of six blocks each as shown. Each row has green (or gray) triangles at the top and every other block is rotated 180°. Join the blocks into vertical rows. Press the seam allowances in opposite directions from row to row. Join the rows as shown in the quilt assembly diagram on page 67. Press the seam allowances in one direction. The quilt top should measure 60½" x 72½".

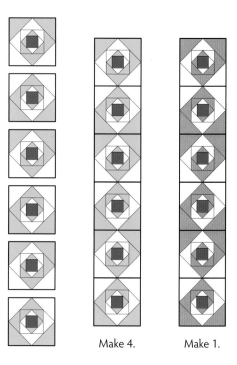

Make 4.   Make 1.

2. Sew the white 72½"-long strips to opposite sides of the quilt center. Press the seam allowances toward the white strips. Sew the white 78½"-long strips to the top and bottom of the quilt top. Press the seam allowances toward the border.

FINISHING THE QUILT

For detailed instructions on finishing techniques, refer to "Finishing Your Quilt" on page 77.

1. Cut and piece the backing fabric so it's 3" to 6" larger than the quilt top. Layer the quilt top with batting and backing. Baste the layers together.

2. Hand or machine quilt as desired. See "Quilting Suggestions," right.

3. Square up the quilt sandwich.

4. Use the red 2½"-wide strips to make and attach the binding.

QUILTING SUGGESTIONS

This project began with a good design, but the quilting made this quilt great. Katie emphasized the vertical gray streak by quilting vertical lines on the blocks. She then countered these lines by creating a few diagonal lines across the blocks and into the borders. A line detail was quilted in the new diagonal sections and a paisley pattern was quilted in the rest of the background, which reflects the pattern on the white fabric. The result is a quilt that has a lot of texture and character.

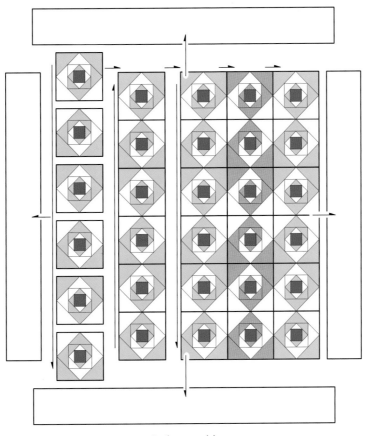

Quilt assembly

■ "Amish Nine Patch," pieced by Myra Harder and quilted by Katie Friesen

AMISH NINE PATCH

The very first quilt block I remember making was a Nine Patch, and the simple joy of sewing more like it kept me entertained for hours. I still love sewing these quick and easy blocks, and I think they look great made in the rich solid colors of the Amish lifestyle.

- **FINISHED QUILT**
  54½" x 65½"

- **FINISHED BLOCK**
  6" x 6"

AMISH TO URBAN
See "Southern Comfort" on page 73 for an urban twist on this Amish quilt.

MATERIALS

Yardage is based on 42"-wide fabric.

2 yards of purple solid for blocks and outer border
1¼ yard of navy solid for sashing, inner border, and binding
¼ yard *each* of red, dark-green, light-green, and dark-teal solids
   for blocks
1 yard of teal solid for blocks and setting triangles
⅔ yard of olive-green solid for setting triangles
3½ yards of fabric for backing
59" x 70" piece of batting

CUTTING

From the *lengthwise* grain of the purple solid, cut:
2 strips, 5½" x 55½"
2 strips, 5½" x 54½"

From the *crosswise* grain of the remaining purple solid, cut:
3 strips, 2½" x 42"

From *each* of the red, dark-green, light-green, and dark-teal
solids, cut:
3 strips, 2½" x 42" (12 total)

From the teal solid, cut:
2 strips, 9¾" x 42"; crosscut into 5 squares, 9¾" x 9¾". Cut into quarters
   diagonally to yield 20 triangles.
4 squares, 5¼" x 5¼"; cut in half diagonally to yield 8 triangles
3 strips, 2½" x 42"

From the olive-green solid, cut:
2 strips, 9¾" x 42"; crosscut into 5 squares, 9¾" x 9¾". Cut into quarters
   diagonally to yield 20 triangles.
4 squares, 5¼" x 5¼"; cut in half diagonally to yield 8 triangles

From the navy solid, cut:
16 strips, 2½" x 42"

MAKING THE BLOCKS

1. Join two purple 2½" x 42" strips and one dark-green strip along their long edges to make a strip set. Press the seam allowances toward the dark-green strip. Crosscut the strip set into 16 segments, 2½" wide.

2½"

Make 1 strip set.
Cut 16 segments.

2. Join two dark-green strips and one purple 2½"-wide strip along their long edges to make a strip set. Press the seam allowances toward the dark-green strips. Crosscut the strip set into eight segments, 2½" wide.

2½"

Make 1 strip set.
Cut 8 segments.

3. Lay out two segments from step 1 and one segment from step 2 as shown. Join the segments to make one green-and-purple block. Make a total of eight blocks.

Make 8.

4. Using the light-green and dark-teal strips, repeat steps 1–3 to make eight blocks. In the same way, use the teal and red strips to make eight blocks.

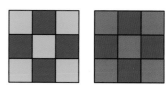

Make 8 of each.

ASSEMBLING THE QUILT TOP

The blocks are assembled in vertical rows, using two blocks of each color combination in each row.

1. Lay out six blocks, 10 teal 9¾" triangles, and four teal 5¼" triangles as shown. Join the blocks into diagonal rows. Press the seam allowances toward the triangles. Join the rows and press the seam allowances in one direction. Add the corner triangles last and press. Trim and square up the row to measure 9" x 51½", making sure to leave ¼" beyond the points of the blocks for seam allowances.

2. Using the remaining teal triangles, repeat step 1 to make a second row. In the same way, use the olive-green triangles to make two rows.

3. Join the navy strips end to end. From the pieced strip, cut five 51½"-long strips and two 44½"-long strips.

4. Join the block rows and three navy 51½"-long strips, alternating them as shown. Press the seam allowances toward the navy strips. The quilt center should measure 40½" x 51½".

Quilt assembly

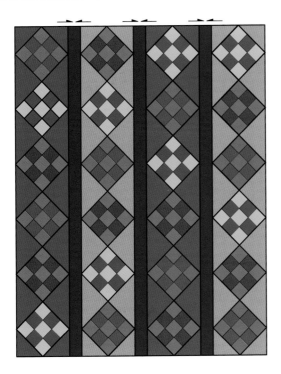

5. Sew navy 51½"-long strips to opposite sides of the quilt center. Press the seam allowances toward the navy strips. Sew navy 44½"-long strips to the top and bottom of the quilt top to complete the inner border. Press the seam allowances toward the inner border.

6. Sew purple 55½"-long strips to opposite sides of the quilt top. Press the seam allowances toward the purple strips. Sew purple 54½"-long strips to the top and bottom of the quilt top. Press the seam allowances toward the outer border.

FINISHING THE QUILT

For detailed instructions on finishing techniques, refer to "Finishing Your Quilt" on page 77.

1. Cut and piece the backing fabric so it's 3" to 6" larger than the quilt top. Layer the quilt top with batting and backing. Baste the layers together.

2. Hand or machine quilt as desired. See "Quilting Suggestions" below.

3. Square up the quilt sandwich.

4. Use the navy 2½" x 54" strips to make and attach the binding.

QUILTING SUGGESTIONS

Curved lines were quilted through the Nine Patch blocks, and the setting triangles were echo quilted. A continuous seed-and-diamond design was quilted in the sashing and inner border. The outer border was quilted with plain lines that reflect the simple lifestyle of the Amish.

■ "Southern Comfort," pieced by Myra Harder and quilted by Katie Friesen

Layer-Cake Friendly!

SOUTHERN COMFORT

I created this quilt because I had a layer cake (package of 10" fabric squares) sitting in my studio that I just couldn't ignore. It's very, very unusual for me to make a quilt without having a detailed plan, but this project created itself as it went along. The result was a warm and inviting quilt that many of my friends are trying to steal for themselves. But that's OK—this project was so enjoyable that I don't mind making more!

- **FINISHED QUILT**
  86" x 107"

- **FINISHED BLOCK**
  13½" x 13½"

URBAN TO AMISH
See "Amish Nine Patch" on page 69 for the Amish inspiration for this urban quilt.

MATERIALS

Yardage is based on 42"-wide fabric.

5⅛ yards of ivory print for blocks, sashing, and border
40 squares, 10" x 10", of assorted prints OR ⅜ yard *each* of 10 assorted prints for blocks
⅝ yard of apricot print for sashing
⅞ yard of yellow print for binding
7¾ yards of fabric for backing
91" x 112" piece of batting

CUTTING

From the ivory print, cut:
13 strips, 5" x 42"; crosscut *3 of the strips* into 20 squares, 5" x 5"
10 strips, 8" x 42"; crosscut into:
    12 squares, 8" x 8"
    62 rectangles, 5" x 8"
12 strips, 2" x 42"

From the assorted prints, cut:
160 squares, 5" x 5" (cut in matching sets of 4; keep like fabrics together)

From the apricot print, cut:
8 strips, 2" x 42"

From the yellow print, cut:
10 strips, 2½" x 42"

MAKING THE BLOCKS

Using four squares *each* of two different prints and one ivory 5" square, lay out the squares in a nine-patch arrangement as shown. Join the squares into rows. Press the seam allowances in the directions indicated. Join the rows and press the seam allowances away from the center square. Make a total of 20 blocks.

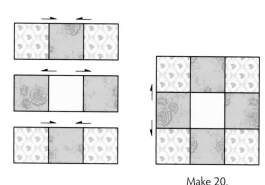

Make 20.

MAKING THE SASHING UNITS

1. Join three ivory 2"-wide strips and two apricot strips along their long edges, alternating the strips as shown to make a strip set. Press the seam allowances toward the apricot strips. Make four strips sets. Cut the strip sets into 31 segments, 5" wide.

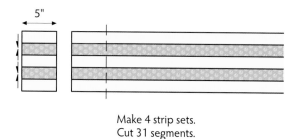

Make 4 strip sets.
Cut 31 segments.

2. Sew ivory 5" x 8" rectangles to opposite sides of each segment to make a sashing unit. Press the seam allowances toward the ivory rectangles. Make 31 units.

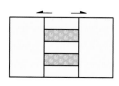

Make 31.

ASSEMBLING THE QUILT TOP

1. Sew together four blocks and three sashing units, alternating them as shown to make a block row. Press the seam allowances toward the blocks. Make five rows.

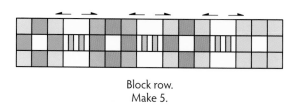

Block row.
Make 5.

2. Sew together four sashing units and three ivory 8" squares, alternating them as shown to make a sashing row. Press the seam allowances toward the ivory squares. Make four rows.

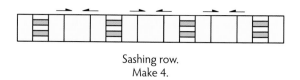

Sashing row.
Make 4.

3. Lay out the block rows and sashing rows as shown in the quilt assembly diagram on page 75. Join the rows and press the seam allowances toward the block rows. The quilt top should measure 77" x 98".

4. Join the 10 ivory 5"-wide strips end to end. From the pieced strip, cut two 98"-long strips and sew them to opposite sides of the quilt center. Press the seam allowances toward the ivory strips.

5. From the remaining pieced strip, cut two 86"-long strips. Sew the strips to the top and bottom of the quilt top to complete the border. Press the seam allowances toward the border.

FINISHING THE QUILT

For detailed instructions on finishing techniques, refer to "Finishing Your Quilt" on page 77.

1. Cut and piece the backing fabric so it's 3" to 6" larger than the quilt top. Layer the quilt top with batting and backing. Baste the layers together.

2. Hand or machine quilt as desired. See "Quilting Suggestions," right.

3. Square up the quilt sandwich.

4. Use the yellow 2½"-wide strips to make and attach the binding.

QUILTING SUGGESTIONS

I wanted the quilting on this project to be gentle and soft. Katie quilted a seed design on each of the large squares and she joined the apricot sashing pieces together with horizontal and vertical quilted lines. The border was quilted with a lazy curving vine that adds just the right amount of grace to the quilt.

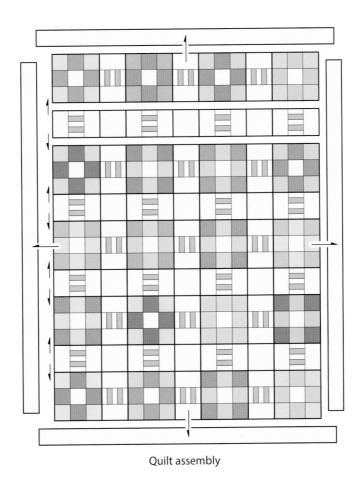

Quilt assembly

FINISHING YOUR QUILT

The end is in sight. Now it's time to layer the quilt top with batting and backing, quilt the layers, and bind the edges. I've included quilting suggestions for each project, but I encourage you to use a design that fits your quilt and the recipient.

BASTING

Before you layer the quilt, press the quilt top and backing carefully. Then spread the backing wrong side up on a flat, clean surface. Anchor the backing with masking tape, taking care not to stretch the fabric out of shape. Center the batting over the backing, smoothing out any wrinkles. Center the quilt top, right side up, over the batting, again smoothing out any wrinkles. Baste the layers with #2 rustproof safety pins. Place the pins 4" to 6" apart. Remove the tape and you're ready to quilt.

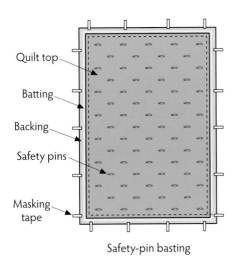

Quilt top

Batting

Backing

Safety pins

Masking
tape

Safety-pin basting

QUILTING

Quilting is what holds the sandwich of fabric and batting together. Traditionally quilting was done by hand, rocking a needle back and forth through all of the layers. Today, quilting is usually done using a sewing machine, which makes the task quicker and allows for intricate patterns.

To quilt using a personal sewing machine, I recommend using two different types of sewing-machine feet. To quilt straight lines, use a walking foot. This foot helps compress the layers and move them evenly through the machine, which helps prevent bunching and pulling. If you want to quilt a free-motion type of design that flows over the entire quilt, you'll need to use a darning foot. Depending on your sewing-machine model, you'll have a darning foot that's either *open toe* or a fully closed round foot. This foot allows you to freely move the fabric in various directions so you can quilt circles and swirls.

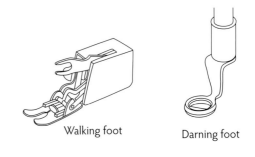

Walking foot   Darning foot

BINDING

When you've finished quilting your project, use a cutting mat, ruler, and rotary cutter to trim your quilt to its finished size. Trim each side so that all three layers (the quilt top, batting, and backing) have straight edges. Now you just need to add a binding or edging to finish the project.

There are a number of ways to bind the edges of your quilt. I prefer to finish my quilts using a double-fold binding made with strips cut 2½"-wide and sewn with a ¼" seam allowance. Cut the required number of strips as instructed for the project.

1. Place two strips at right angles, right sides together. Draw a diagonal line on the top strip and stitch along the line as shown.

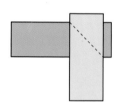

2. Trim the seam allowance to ¼". Press the seam allowances open. Add the remaining strips in the same manner to make one long strip.

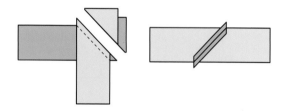

3. When all of the strips have been joined, cut one end at a 45° angle. This will be the beginning of the strip. Press the strip in half lengthwise, wrong sides together and raw edges aligned.

4. Beginning with the angled end, place the binding strip along one edge of the right side of the quilt. Starting several inches away from a corner, align the raw edges of the strip with the quilt-top edge. Leaving 8" at the beginning of the strip unstitched, use a ¼" seam allowance to stitch the binding to the quilt. Stop stitching ¼" from the corner and backstitch.

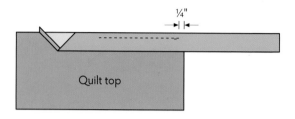

5. Remove the quilt from the sewing machine. Turn the quilt so you're ready to sew the next side. Fold the binding straight up, away from the quilt, to create a 45°-angle fold. Fold the binding back down onto itself, even with the edge of the quilt top, to create an angled pleat at the corner. Beginning at the edge, stitch the binding to the quilt, stopping ¼" from the next corner. Repeat the process on the remaining corners of the quilt.

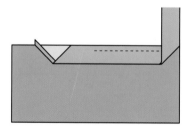

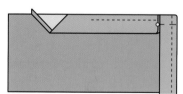

6. When you're 8" to 12" away from your starting point, stop stitching and remove the quilt from the machine. Cut the end of the binding strip so it overlaps the beginning of the binding strip by at least 5". Pin the ends together 3½" from the starting point. Clip the binding raw edges at the pin, being careful not to cut past the seam allowance or into the quilt layers. Open up the binding and match the clipped edges as shown, right sides together. Stitch the binding strips together on the diagonal.

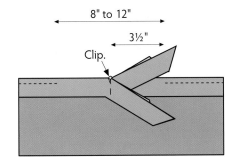

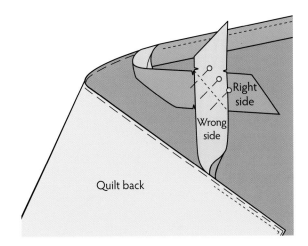

7. Refold the binding and check to make sure it fits the quilt. Trim the binding ends, leaving a ¼" seam allowance. Press the seam allowances open. Finish stitching the binding to the quilt top.

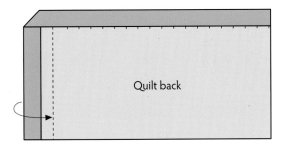

8. Fold the binding to the back of the quilt. Using matching thread and making sure the machine stitching line is covered, hand stitch the folded edge to the backing. Fold the binding to form a miter at each corner.

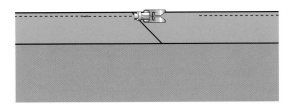

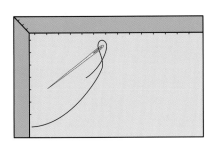

ACKNOWLEDGMENTS

The quilts in this book would not be what they are without the help of an expert machine quilter. I am very grateful to Katie Friesen, who enthusiastically tackled each quilt. Katie has a long background in hand quilting, so I knew she would be the perfect quilter to understand the styles and designs of traditional Amish quilts. It was also fun to talk about new imaginative quilting ideas for the modern projects. Thank you, Katie, for sharing your talents—and for knowing the deadline and still saying, "Of course we can do it!"

I'm thankful to my mother, Betty Klassen, who expertly pieced some of the projects in this book.

I'm very grateful to all of the editors at Martingale who polished my ideas and the design team who turned them into a beautiful finished book. Thank you for making my ideas shine.

ABOUT THE AUTHOR

MYRA HARDER has been working in the quilting and textile industry for the past two decades, and has found herself on the same path as her forefathers: her family ties can be traced back nine generations to fabric merchants in Prussia in the mid 1600s.

Myra loves designing quilts, and her designs have been featured in books of quilt patterns as well as in countless magazines. She also designs fabric. In the future, she hopes to continue creating and producing new ideas to inspire the next generation.

She lives in Winkler, Manitoba, Canada, with her husband, Mark, and their two children, Samson and Robyn.